TWO FACE

TWO FACE

This book is a work of fiction. Names, character, places and incidents are a product of the author's imagination or are fictitious. Any resemblance to actual events or locales or persons living or dead is entirely coincidental

© 2013 by Tracey Ferguson

All rights reserved, including the right to reproduce this book or portions thereof in any form whatsoever. For information contact Ferguson Publishing Co. at info@traeferguson.com

ISBN-13-978-0615925004
ISBN-10-0615925006

Author: Trae Ferguson
Cover Design/ Graphic Designer: Gregory Graphics
Editing: English Ruler
Formatting by Lashawone Powell

Printed in the USA 2013

Acknowledgements

I want to thank God first and foremost for waking me up every day and blessing me with a gift that allows me to entertain, educate, motivate, and inspire others.

I would also like thank my biggest supporters, my friends and coworkers at Mercy Medical Center. There are too many to name, but there are a few people who go above and beyond. Stacie Merrit, Cambria Donovan, Darlene Brown, Lakeisha Thomas, Larry Cross, Nickia Trafton, and my boss Deborah Young, thank you for allowing me to take off so I can attend book signings and other events.

To my beautiful sista's thank you for your support, encouragement and love.

Thanks to the following book clubs and radio/blog shows: Chi-town Reading Circle, Readers with Attitudes (RWA), Delicious Talk, Sistahs on Lit, and I saved the best for last, the best book club in the

TWO FACE

game ARC Book Club, Inc and The 1Essence Radio Show, thank you for all your love and support.

My fellow authors who have inspired and encouraged me along the way, The1Essence and Author Brooklen Borne without you Sweet 16 would still be hiding in my notebook. English Ruler and Nikkea Smithers, I have grown as a writer because of your advice and encouraging words. Loretta R. Walls, Envy Red, Rahiem Brooks, Author David L, Author Ladeaux, Rickey Teems, J.W. Smith, Tanisha Pettiford, J'son Lee and Manswell Peterson, I watch and learn from the best. Love you all.

To my readers, I love and appreciate all of you, without you there would be no Author Trae Ferguson. A special thank you to some readers who also go above and beyond to show me love, Nicole Williams, MeLissa Manual, Debbie Burnett, Debi Delano, Nikki Burrell, SiStar Tea, Ivy Dixion, Qiana Drennen and my girl Author LaRedeaux aka Redbone. You show me mad support daily, I love you for life.

☿

To Gregory Graphics who took my vision of my book cover and turned it into a work of art.

Another special shout out to English Ruler and LaRedeaux for all their help and support during this project. Love you both.

To my true love, Joseph, you are the reason I do everything because you are my everything.

To the love of my life Dana Henson, thank you loving and accepting me as I am. Thank you for supporting my dream and always being right by my side.

Dedication

I dedicate this book to anyone who has to fight every day to be accepted by family, friends, and society just because you're different.

God Bless you all.

CHAPTER ONE

Diane and Kristopher Michaels had been happily married for little over five years and longed for a child to complete their family. After two devastating miscarriages they thought this day would never come.

On May 22, 1987 Diane and Kristopher Michaels became the proud parents of a healthy baby boy, Kristopher Jr. He weighed in at a whopping nine pounds, ten ounces and twenty-two inches long with ten little fingers and ten little toes. He was a beautiful sight and a dream come true for the proud father. All he ever wanted was a son.

As he held his namesake in his arms for the first time, a wide grin spread across his face.

TWO FACE

Daydreaming about the many father/son moments they would soon share, little did he know in just a few years his dreams would be shattered.

Five years later...

By the time little Kristopher was five years old it was obvious that something was different about him. Whenever he would play with other children he would always choose to play with the dolls instead of the cars or trucks. At first his parents didn't make it an issue until one day Diane got the shock of her life as she entered their bedroom and found him playing with her makeup. He sat there with rosy cheeks, which was compliments of his mother's blush, and was applying lipstick as his mother entered the room.

"Kristopher, what are you doing in my make up?" she asked trying to hide how upset she really was.

⚧

"I want to be pretty like you mommy," he said with an innocent smile as he turned and looked at her.

"Kristopher, little boys are handsome and my little man is definitely handsome, just like his daddy," she stated with a calm but concerned tone.

"I want to be pretty like you," Kristopher shot back, this time with an attitude.

"Let's go in the bathroom and get you cleaned up before daddy gets home," Diane pleaded with Kristopher as he began to throw a tantrum on the floor.

"No mommy, I want daddy to see how pretty I look," Kristopher Jr. cried. Diane knew it would break her husband's heart to see his son that way.

"Kristopher Daniel Michaels get in this bathroom and clean yourself up now!" Diane yelled. Even at a young age Kristopher knew when his mother said his whole name she meant business. He stomped his way into the bathroom and with his mother's help removed all traces of the makeup, he then went to his room where he cried his self to sleep. Just as Diane closed the door to her son's bedroom, she heard her husband coming in the front door. She took a sigh of relief that she was able to save her husband some heartache, at least for the moment. She knew she had to tell him, but seeing it would have been too much for him to bear.

As she went downstairs to greet her husband she searched for the right words to tell her husband what had just happened.

"Hello beautiful how was your day?" he asked followed by a kiss. Kristopher had a very successful construction company, which allowed Diane to be a stay at home mom.

"Sweetie we need to talk about Kristopher," she replied as little beads of sweat formed above her top lip.

"What's wrong, is he sick?" he asked with concern.

"Kris today, well actually about twenty minutes before you got home, I walked in on KJ.

playing in my makeup," she blurted out before she lost the nerve.

"So what's the big deal Diane? He's just curious."

"Kris...he was wearing it," she said as she watched her husband's heartbreak before her very eyes.

"What?" he asked as he fell back in the chair placing his hand across his forehead.

"I walked in our bedroom and K.J. was wearing my blush and applying my lipstick. When I asked him what he was doing he said, "I want to look pretty like you mommy." Kris I'm worried and judging by the shocked look on your face I can see that this concerns you as well," Diane stated as she gently rubbed the back of her husband's head. Still stunned by his wife's words, Kristopher just sat there speechless. "Honey, please say something," Diane pleaded. "Wow." That was the only word that escaped his lips followed by a single tear. As the single tear fell, the sound of small footsteps echoed from above. KJ had woken up from his catnap after hearing the sound of his father's voice and ran downstairs eager to see him.

"Hi daddy", KJ. said as he leapt in his father's arms and hugged him tight.

"Hey little man," his father said as his voice cracked and the rest of his tears were released.

"What's wrong daddy, why are you crying?" KJ asked as he wiped his father's tears.

"Nothing little man, I just love you so much. All I ever wanted was you, a son and I will love you no matter what." Diane let them have their moment but soon joined in.

"Group hug," she said as she embraced the two most important people in her life, wondering if she made too much of what K.J. did or was it a sign of something more.

"Little man, I need to finish talking to daddy, can you go upstairs in your room and play. I promise we won't be much longer," said Diane.

⚥

"Yes mommy."

"Kris, I'm so sorry. Maybe I'm making more out of this than it really is. He's only a baby and like you said they are curious at this age," Diane said trying to convince herself that her motherly instinct was wrong.

"I hope your right sweetheart."

∞∞∞∞∞∞

Months had passed without incident, which put Kristopher and Diane both at ease until two weeks before Halloween when Diane decided to take K.J. shopping for his costume. Every year her sister Cheryl gave a big Halloween party at her house. Everyone dressed up in costumes, even the adults. The kids played games, bobbed for apples and a good time was had by all.

When they arrived at Party City, K.J. was practically dragging his mother down the aisle where the costumes were.

TWO FACE

"Okay honey, do you want to be Spiderman or Batman?" she asked as she held up both costumes excited to see which he would chose, but K.J. had his eye on something else.

"Mommy, I want to be a princess," he said as he took the pretty pink costume off the rack and handed it to his mother. Diane's fair skin turned beat red as she dropped the costumes, grabbed K.J. by the hand and ran out the store.

"Mommy, why are we leaving?" K.J. asked with tears in his big brown eyes. He was too young to understand how disturbing his behavior was to his mother. "You forgot my costume mommy," he whined. Diane never said a word; she just drove home in silence with tears streaming down her face as she wondered what was wrong with her baby boy.

Diane thought if she just ignored the situation that it would just go away, but she would soon find out that the situation would only get worse. After the incident at Party City, K.J.'s behavior changed

⚥

dramatically. He became withdrawn and appeared to be depressed. Diane and Kristopher decided to go to the Halloween party hoping it would cheer KJ. up.

"Come on KJ., it's time to go to the party," Diane yelled from the bottom of the stairs. "I hope this cheers him up. He has been so sad lately," she said as she turned to face her husband.

"I'm sure it will do him some good to be around the family," Kristopher replied.

KJ. slowly walked down the stairs with his head hung low. As he approached the bottom of the stairs he looked up at his mother with sadness in his eyes and asked, "Why are we going to a Halloween party in our regular clothes?"

Diane gently lifted her son's chin and replied, "We are going as ourselves and that's better than any costume we could wear."

"It doesn't matter anyway because I always feel like I'm wearing a costume," KJ. said, as he looked his mother in her eyes. Diane turned and looked at her husband as they both were stunned by the words of their five-year-old son. Once again they ignored their son's cries for help and made their way to the party.

∞∞∞∞∞∞

Everyone was having a great time at the party, even K.J. It put Diane and Kristopher's mind at ease to see him laughing and playing with his cousins. Just as they let their guard down, Diane heard all the kids laughing and calling K.J. names. She ran in the basement to see what was going on with her husband Kristopher not far behind. What they saw stopped them dead in their tracks.

"Look mommy and daddy, I'm a princess," he said as he twirled around in the pretty pink costume that he had gotten from his cousin Amber. Kristopher picked up his son as Diane gathered their belongings and they ran out of the party without as much as a good bye.

The ride home was quiet with the exception of K.J. crying in the back seat. Diane and Kristopher spoke volumes without saying a word as they held hands and occasionally looked into each other's teary eyes. One thing that was certain; they knew it was time to seek professional help for their son.

CHAPTER TWO

Diane wasted no time looking for the perfect therapist so they could find out exactly what they were dealing with as far as K.J. was concerned. In her search she ran across The Center for Child and Family Therapy located right in Owings Mills. She was very impressed with the credentials of one doctor on site, Dr. Paul Stevenson, who came highly recommended and was said to be excellent with children. Her hand shook as she reached for the phone to make the appointment. In her heart she knew that this phone call could change their lives forever.

∞∞∞∞∞∞

"Sweetheart, we have an appointment today with Dr. Stevenson. I don't want you to be afraid, daddy and I will be right there with you," Diane explained.

"Why am I going to the doctors, I'm not sick mommy," K.J. asked with a raised brow.

"I know honey; Dr Stevenson is a different kind of doctor. He is a therapist, people go to a therapist when they need someone to talk to about what they are feeling and in this case Dr. Stevenson talks to children about their feelings," she said searching her son's eyes for understanding.

"Okay mommy."

"Are you two ready? I don't want to be late for our first appointment," Kristopher said upon entering the room.

"Relax honey; we're only going to Owing Mills, besides we both are ready to go.

They arrived at Dr. Stevenson's office at 9:45 sharp with fifteen minutes to spare, just enough time for their nerves to kick in. However they began to relax as the bright colorful décor of the office was very warm and inviting not to mention kid friendly with stuffed animals and toys for kids of all ages. It even had a Sega Genesis for the older kids.

When KJ saw the toys he ran straight to the dolls instead of the so called "boy toys." Diane and Kristopher just looked at each other and hoped this appointment would give them some answers.

"Mr. and Mrs. Michaels, Dr. Stevenson is ready to see you now," said the tall skinny receptionist.

"Come on KJ. it's time to see the Dr.," Diane said as she reached out her hand. KJ. got up and ran to his mother. Diane could tell by his tight grip and sweaty palm that he was nervous.

"Remember what I told you sweetie, your dad and I are right here, so just relax and answer the doctor's question as best you can."

They stepped into a small office and were greeted by short brawny man wearing black-framed glasses.

"Hello Mr. and Mrs. Michaels, I am Dr. Stevenson," he said with his hand extended.

"Hello, I am Kristopher and this is my wife Diane and our son Kristopher Jr. but we call him K.J.," replied Kristopher as they shook hands.

"Do you mind if I call you K.J. young man?" asked Dr. Stevenson as he rubbed the top of K.J.'s head.

"No, I don't mind Mr. Doctor," K.J. said causing them all to laugh.

"Okay K.J., I would like to talk to your mom and dad first, so would you mind going in the playroom. We won't be long, I promise."

"Okay."

"Don't worry I can see everything he is doing on this monitor. It helps to put the parents at ease as well as help me see behavioral problems if there are any. From reading the forms you filled out I see that K.J. is displaying homosexual behavior. Now what has he done for you to come to that conclusion?"

TWO FACE

"Well Dr. Stevenson there has been a few incidents. First, I caught him putting on my makeup and then when we went shopping for his Halloween costume and he wanted to be a princess instead of batman or Spiderman. Even though I decided not to buy him a costume, he didn't let that stop him. He put on his cousin Amber's princess costume at the party and as you can see on your monitor he likes playing with dolls instead of trucks like normal little boys," Diane stated as she lost the battle with the tears she fought so hard to hold back.

"I want you both to be honest with me as well as yourselves with this next question I am about to ask you. Would it matter to you if K.J. was gay?" Dr. Stevenson asked with his legs crossed and index finger resting on his temple.

"Diane quickly replied, "I will love my son no matter what." They both turned to Kristopher waiting for his response, but all they got was silent tears. "Kristopher that is your son and you should love and accept him no matter what, "Diane said shocked by his silence.

☿

"I understand your pain Kristopher, but I must warn you it could be something far worse than him being gay and if you can't handle that then I am almost certain that you won't be able to handle the other alternative. I would like to talk to your son before I say anything else." The doctor asked his receptionist to walk Diane and Kristopher back to the waiting area so he could talk to K.J. alone.

"K.J. your mom and dad are right outside. Now it's time for us to get to know each other a little better. The first thing I want you to do is draw me a picture of how you see yourself.

"Okay," K.J. responded with a wide grin as Dr. Stevenson handed him some paper and crayons and patiently waited for K.J. to unveil his masterpiece.

When K.J. was finished he jumped up excited to show the doctor the drawing of himself.

"Here's my picture Dr. Stevenson," he said grinning proudly from ear to ear.

"Okay, let's see what we have here," replied the doctor as K.J. handed him the drawing. His forehead wrinkled as his suspicions were confirmed. K.J. drew a picture of a little girl wearing a pretty pink dress with a pink hair bow to match.

"Very good K.J, I want to ask you a few questions before I bring your parents back in, if that's ok with you?"

"Yes."

"Why did you draw yourself as a little girl?"

"Because I am a girl on the inside, but I look like a boy on the outside," K.J. explained.

"Does this make you feel sad?"

"Yes, I don't want to be a boy, but it makes my mom and dad sad when I try to be a girl."

"You did a great job, but I think it's time we let your parents join us, "Dr. Stevenson said as he gently patted K.J. on his back. He buzzed his receptionist and told her to send in Diane and Kristopher.

⚥

"Hello sweetheart, did you have fun with Dr. Stevenson?" Diane asked as her eyes shifted from her son and then back to the doctor.

"Yes mommy I drew a picture of myself," he said with pride.

"Well let me see this masterpiece." Dr. Stevenson handed her the drawing without any warning and watched as Diane and Kristopher looked at the picture their son had drawn.

"I don't understand. Is this a picture of you in your Halloween costume?" she asked in confusion. Meanwhile, Kristopher looked at the picture and turned his back.

"No mommy, when I look in the mirror I look like a girl, but to you I look like a boy."

"What the hell is going on here? He doesn't know what he's talking about, he's only five years old for God sakes!" Kristopher yelled.

"K.J. why don't you go back in the playroom so I can talk to your parents."

"Okay," K.J. said as he walked away in sadness.

"Mr. and Mrs. Michaels please sit down so I can help you understand what your son is trying to tell you," Dr. Stevenson pleaded. Your son has a gender identity disorder, which means he is not gay; he is not a five year old cross dresser. He is trapped in the wrong body. His mind and body are in a constant battle with one another. Physically he looks like a boy, while his mind is telling him he is a girl."

Diane and Kristopher cried in each other's arms as they listened to the heartbreaking words that were unleashed by the good doctor. They knew from this moment on their lives were forever changed.

"So what are we supposed to do about this?" asked Kristopher.

"When children with this disorder are forced to live as something that they are not, they become depressed and withdrawn and often times commit suicide. So the question is do you want a live daughter or a dead son?

⚥

CHAPTER THREE

It had been two weeks since their visit to Dr. Stevenson's office and Diane and Kristopher's once happy marriage was crumbling right before their eyes. Kristopher's behavior changed and not for the best. He was hurt and confused, but most of all he was angry.

"I thought God didn't make mistakes; well what in the hell do you call this? All I ever wanted was a son to carry on the Michaels name and now that I have one, he wants to be my daughter. You tell me God, how I'm I suppose to deal with this!" Kristopher ranted to himself in anger.

"Kris lower your voice before K.J. hears you," Diane whispered as she entered the room and closed the door behind her.

"That's all anyone cares about is how he feels or should I say she." Diane's jaw dropped from the comment Kris made and without hesitation she slapped him so hard he dropped the glass of Hennessey he was holding.

"How dare you say such a thing about our child! You should feel blessed to have one regardless of what sex it is. Did you forget how devastating it was to lose two babies before we were blessed with K.J.? I don't know about you, but I refuse to lose another child," Diane said before exiting the room.

Kristopher stood there staring at the beautiful photograph of his family that rested on the nightstand next to his bed. In a fit of rage he knocked it to the floor and watched as it broke into pieces much like the dreams he had for him and his son.

As Diane was running to the bedroom to see what was going on, Kristopher was coming out, nearly knocking her down. He stormed out of the house and jumped into the truck.

Diane ran to the door to try to stop him, but all she saw were the skid marks he left behind. She closed the door, fell to her knees, and prayed for her family.

∞∞∞∞∞∞

After driving around for what seemed to be hours Kristopher decided to stop by Corinthians to have a few drinks. He sat at the bar and ordered two shots of Hennessey and told the bartender to keep them coming. He was hoping the more he drank the longer he could forget about his problems at home.

Four shots later, Kristopher was feeling no pain when he was approached by this beautiful woman. She had hair like fire with skin that looked like it was kissed by the sun and a sexy mole right above her naturally pouty lips.

"Hey handsome, don't you think you should slow down a bit?" she asked as she rested her hand on top of his.

"This is your business because..?" he asked.

"I'm making it my business. Would you like me to take you home or would you like to go to my place?" she asked in a seductive tone while twirling the keys on her index finger.

"Your place," Kristopher said as he paid his tab and left with the beautiful stranger. Looking for any escape from his own reality he decided to participate in a little fantasy.

With alcohol in full control of his actions Kristopher didn't wait until they got to the house of the woman whose name he didn't know. He caressed her breasts and pinched her nipples and it became harder for her to keep her eyes on the road.

She found a dark secluded spot and pulled over as he touched her body and craved for much more.

She crawled over to the passenger's seat and straddled him like a horse. While playing in his curly black hair she traced his lips with her tongue and he welcomed it in his mouth. They shared a long passionate kiss as if they were long lost lovers. He could feel the warmth of her wet pussy as it rested on his lap.

"Oh my God, your pussy is so wet," he said as he lifted her skirt and removed her thong. He placed two fingers inside of her while she pulled out her right breast and rubbed her nipple across his lips. He finger fucked her until her juices began to run down his hand.

"Yessss!" she screamed as she creamed all over his hand and he licked each finger one by one.

"Oh you nasty just the way I like it," she said with a look of satisfaction.

"Let's go to your place so I can show you how nasty I can be."

"Your wish is my command," she said returning to the driver's seat and starting the engine. "By the way my name is Sherry, but everyone calls me Reds."

TWO FACE

It wasn't until then that he realized he didn't know anything about this woman, but that didn't seem to stop him from making what would soon be the biggest mistake of his life.

"So do you have a name handsome?" she asked smiling.

"Kris," he responded as he admired the beautiful creature before him.

Just fifteen minutes later they arrived at her apartment. "Here we are, welcome to my home and make yourself comfortable." With every step she took she took off a piece of clothing that led him to her bedroom. He followed the trail of clothing and when he entered the bedroom Reds was lying across the bed waiting for him.

Kris couldn't resist and for the second time that night he broke his wedding vows. Diane and Kristopher had been together for a total of thirteen years and married for ten of them. Kristopher had never thought of being with another woman, but he allowed his pain that was now mixed with alcohol to push him to a point of no return.

Meanwhile, Diane is at home sick with worry. She called all his friends, family and even the hospitals trying to find her husband. She knew how angry he was not to mention he had been drinking. Something he had been doing a lot since their visit to Dr. Stevenson's office.

She knew how important having a son was to Kristopher, but she didn't understand why he didn't share that unconditional love she had for K.J. As difficult as it was for her, she would do whatever it took to make sure her child was happy. She was very disappointed in Kristopher's selfishness. He was only concerned about what he wanted.

"Please God, let my husband be safe and unharmed," she prayed with tears pouring from her eyes.

"Mommy I'm hungry," K.J. said as he swung open her bedroom door. "Where's daddy?"

TWO FACE

That was a good question, she thought to herself. Kristopher had never stayed out all night unless he was away on business and her womanly instinct was telling her otherwise.

"Mommy why are you crying, did I do something to make you sad again,"

She grabbed her son and held him close. "Sweetheart, you make my heart smile. Please don't ever think that. Now go wash up, I'm going to make you pancakes for breakfast."

After KJ closed the door, she decided to try calling Kristopher again. It just rang and rang, but as she was about to hang up she heard someone saying hello.

"Hello Kris," Diane spoke into the phone.

"Hello." Diane dropped the phone when she realized the voice at the other end was not Kris, but that of a woman.

∞∞∞∞∞∞

As the sunlight danced across his face Kristopher woke up from a deep sleep in a panic when reality hit him. It wasn't until that very moment that he realized that he had been out all night.

"Damn, what time is it? Have you seen my phone?" he asked as he looked around the room for his phone.

Reds turned to him and lied with a straight face, "Its right here where you left it." She picked up his phone and handed it to him.

Kristopher looked at her in confusion. "I could have sworn I put it over here last night." He looked at his phone and noticed the twenty missed calls and several voicemails that Diane left for him.

I can only imagine what's going on inside that pretty little head of hers, he thought to himself. He jumped up picking his clothes up off the floor and got dressed.

"Sherry can you please drive me back to my truck? I really need to get home now."

TWO FACE

"Of course handsome, just let me freshen up a bit," she replied as she made her way to the bathroom. She stood there looking at herself in the mirror when a devilish grin came across her face as she replayed Diane's voice in her head.

The knock on the door interrupted her thoughts. "Coming sweetie," she said as she took a quick bird bath and threw on some sweats and a tee shirt.

The ride back to Corinthians was short and silent as Kristopher stared out the window thinking how quickly his dream turned into a nightmare.

"Thanks Sherry, take care of yourself," Kristopher said as he exited the truck as if the night they shared never happened.

"Any...." was all she could get out before Kristopher slammed the door, jumped in his truck and once again sped off. Ok, I'm going to let that slide this time, but we will meet again.

Reds pulled off slowly, plotting as she drove.

☿

When Kristopher got home Diane's car was not in the driveway. He opened the door and called out her name as he ran through the house looking for her and K.J. When he reached the bedroom he noticed a note lying across his pillow.

Kris,

What happened to for better or worse?

Diane

CHAPTER FOUR

As Diane drove away from her beautiful home in Randallstown she was overwhelmed with emotions. Thoughts of the possibility of Kris being unfaithful were front and center. His recent behavior along with the woman answering his phone was confirmation that he no longer wanted to be a part of their family.

She went to her sister Cheryl's house where she was welcomed with open arms, but knew she would have some explaining to do since she hadn't told anyone what was going on at home.

"Come on in Sweetie and make yourselves at home," Cheryl said as she opened the door.

☿

"Thanks Sissy, I appreciate you letting us stay here until I figure things out."

"Hi Aunt Cheryl," K.J. said hugging her tight.

"Hey nephew, why don't you go upstairs with Amber so me and your mommy can talk," Cheryl said dying to know what was going on. As soon as K.J. was out of sight Cheryl wasted no time interrogating Diane.

"What the hell is going on Diane? Why did you leave Kris? I haven't really talked to you since the Halloween party when you guys ran out of here like the house was on fire."

"Sissy, if someone would have told me a few years ago that my world would be turned upside down I would have called them a liar, but here I am. In the last few months I have been dealing with something that I could have never even imagined and unfortunately it has torn my family apart," Diane spoke with tears in her eyes.

"What the hell happened?" Cheryl asked eagerly.

"K.J. has a gender identity disorder which basically means he's physically a little boy but he has a mind of a little girl. He is trapped in the wrong body," Diane confessed as the tears she tried so hard to hold on to were finally released. Cheryl stood there with an open mouth as her baby sister shared her family's secret.

"What, you got all this just because he put on Amber's costume at the Halloween party?" Cheryl asked in disbelief.

"No, there were a few other incidents before then, but after that we knew it was time to take him to see a therapist. The therapist basically told us that we could either have a living healthy daughter or a dead son."

"Are you serious? He actually said that? So I'm assuming Kris isn't taking this too well since you are here."

"No not at all. He has been drinking a lot and hanging out more than usual and last night he didn't bother to come home at all," Diane explained as her sorrow turned into anger.

"Di, I know what you're thinking, but maybe he was too drunk to drive home and stayed at a buddy's house."

"Buddy my ass, when I called him this morning a woman answered his phone and that only confirmed what my gut was already telling me. Mama always told us there is nothing stronger than a woman's intuition. When your gut is trying to tell you something you better listen and let's just say my gut was screaming at me last night."

"Wow baby sis, I'm so sorry you had to deal with all of this alone, but you could have come to me," Cheryl replied as she wiped her sister's tears.

"Thanks Sissy, but I was too embarrassed to tell anyone and the one person I thought I could depend on has turned his back on his family. All he is thinking about is his pain and his loss. I don't think he has thought about what K.J. is going through at all. It's all about him."

TWO FACE

"What are you going to do Diane?"

"What any good mother would do. From the first day I felt him kick I loved him unconditionally and I knew there was nothing in this world I wouldn't do for my child. After losing two babies before him there is no way in hell I'm willing to take a chance on losing another one especially for my own selfish reasons. So I'm going to start a new life with my daughter.

∞∞∞∞∞∞

After reading the note Diane left behind Kristopher laid back on the bed with both arms resting behind his head and stared at the ceiling as the tears rolled from the corners of his eyes. He then jumped up, dropped to his knees searching for guidance and forgiveness.

"God, please forgive me for I have sinned. I have committed adultery and abandoned my family for my own selfish reasons. I am truly ashamed of how I feel, but I feel if I walk away now it would be better for everyone. There is no way I can watch my only son, my namesake become my daughter. God, please forgive me," Kristopher pleaded.

∞∞∞∞∞∞

A week had past and still no word from Kristopher and Diane wasn't about to reach out to him. Everyday K.J. would ask her when they were going home, but she wasn't ready to tell her five year old the truth. Her older sister Cheryl made sure they were both comfortable and was in no rush for them to leave. She enjoyed them being there and it reminded her of when they were kids. After their mother lost her battle to Breast Cancer when Diane was only ten and Cheryl was ten years older, she raised Diane, so the two of them have always been close. Cheryl knew when Diane made up her mind about something it was a done deal.

"Sis, after we drop the kids off at school tomorrow I want you to go with me to look at few townhouses and condos in Columbia and the White Marsh area," Diane said as she sipped on a hot cup of coffee.

"Diane there's no rush, you and K.J. can stay as long as you want," Cheryl replied.

"I know and I have loved being here, but it's time for me and my daughter to move on."

"Ok do you need any help, I mean financially?" asked Cheryl.

"No, I'm good. I still have my inheritance that mom left me," Diane said with a slight giggle.

"After all these years you still have money left?" Cheryl asked with her hand resting on her hip.

"Some, I have all of it. I have never touched it and Kristopher doesn't know anything about it. You remember what momma always told us. 'It doesn't matter how many days of sunshine you have, the rain is sure to come.' Well the heavens have opened and it's raining cats and dogs." They both laughed.

∞∞∞∞∞∞

Diane found the perfect townhouse in White Marsh that had an elementary school right around the corner from their house. It was perfect for her and Kristopher Jr. who will now be going by the name Krisette to start their new life together. Diane was convinced that if she moved K.J. to an area where no one knew them the transition from male to female would be easy, but unfortunately she was wrong.

She stopped getting K.J.'s haircut so it would grow and she could give it a more feminine hairstyle. She went shopping and bought him lots of dresses in his favorite color, which of course was pink. She taught K.J. how to act more like a girl, which wasn't hard because he was already very feminine. The biggest challenge was trying to get him to sit down and pee because he would always forget and stand up. Diane wasn't totally comfortable with what she was doing, but her child's happiness and well-being was all that mattered to her.

She watched her child transition from being a depressed and withdrawn little boy into a happy, energetic little girl. It was like watching a caterpillar transform into a beautiful butterfly. This made Diane feel confident that she had made the right decision in leaving Kristopher and allowing K.J. to live freely as a female.

∞∞∞∞∞∞

It was Krisette's first day at her new school and they both were excited and nervous all at the same time. Diane got up and helped her daughter put on her pretty pink dress with the matching head band that pulled her long curly locks away from her face. After they ate a healthy breakfast, Diane and Krisette walked hand and hand to the school. Diane went in to meet the teacher and then waved good bye to her daughter. Her heart pounded with fear as she walked back home praying every step of the way.

Krisette didn't waste any time making friends and everyone seem to like her right away. She was enjoying her first day at school; that is until the class made a stop to the restroom after lunch. One by one they went into the stalls to use the restroom. As Krisette went to the stall forgetting to lock it behind her, a little girl pushed open the door and saw

Krisette standing there peeing with her panties around her ankles and penis in hand.

"Ewww, Krisette has a penis!" the little girl screamed causing everyone to gather around her stall. Krisette tried to get out, but they pushed her down and begin to beat her until the teacher came in and stopped them.

∞∞∞∞∞∞

Diane panicked when she saw the school's number come across the caller id. She didn't even bother to answer; she ran out the front door and around the corner to the school in fear of what might have happened. When she walked into the principal's office she could not believe her eyes. Krisette's pretty pink dress was covered in blood.

"Sweetheart what happened, did you have a nose bleed?" Diane asked as her top lip began to quiver.

"No mommy I got into a fight in the bathroom," Krisette replied with tears in her eyes.

"A fight!" Diane yelled just as the principal was approaching.

"Mrs. Michaels, I'm Mrs. Paige the principal, please come into my office so we can discuss this in private."

"I just dropped my daughter off a few hours ago and now she is covered in blood. What the hell is going on?"

"Please calm down Mrs. Michaels I totally understand why you're upset and have you every right to be but to be honest, I feel that you need to take some responsibility also. After all you were the one who sent your son to school dressed like a girl. Did you really think you would get away with this?" Principal Paige boldly stated.

Diane was so shocked by Mrs. Paige's words that she just grabbed Krisette by the hand and left the building. On the way home she asked Krisette what happened and she replied, "I forgot to sit on the toilet again." From the moment on Krisette was home schooled.

⚥

CHAPTER FIVE

"K.J.!" Kristopher yelled out as he woke up from a bad dream out of breath with beads of sweat resting on his forehead.

Although he hadn't talked to Diane or his son in almost two months he immediately picked up the phone to make sure everything was ok. Kristopher loved his wife and son very much, but he knew in his heart that he couldn't deal with the reality of the situation. As the phone began to ring he became even more nervous, after all he never even called after reading the note Diane left for him.

"Hello," Diane answered shocked to see her husband's name appear on the screen of her cell phone.

"Diane is everything ok, I had a dream that something happened to K.J. and just wanted to make sure he was ok," Kristopher blurted out without taking a breath.

Diane decided not to tell her husband about the fight on the first day of school because that would only convince him that he was right and she was wrong. At the end of the day it wasn't about who was right and who was wrong, it's about her child living a happy, healthy life.

"Wow it's been almost two months since we have seen or heard from you and now you're concerned about your child. You have some nerve Kristopher Michaels."

"Have you been getting the checks that I've been sending to Cheryl's house?"

"Are you serious? I don't need or want your damn money. Your child needs a father that can love and accept him for who he is."

"As I recall you were the one that left," Kristopher shouted back. Look I didn't call to argue with you, I just wanted to make sure my son was alright."

"You damn right I left your cheating ass!" Diane yelled.

"What the hell are you talking about?" Kristopher asked wondering how she knew about his night with the beautiful redhead.

"Oh, I guess your girlfriend failed to mention that I called huh? By the way your daughter is fine and her name is Krisette!" Diane yelled before disconnecting the call.

Kristopher just sat there with his head in his hands in disbelief of what he just heard. A single tear fell from his eye as he realized that his only son and namesake was now his daughter, Krisette Michaels.

∞∞∞∞∞∞

Sherry stood in front of the full length mirror with a pillow underneath her shirt wondering what she would look like in the months to come. She removed the pillow and rubbed her belly and spoke to the fetus growing inside of her.

"I can't wait to tell your daddy all about you," she said with a wide grin.

Three months earlier...

Sherry Louden, the beautiful woman with the flaming red hair and a body to die for was single with no kids and enjoyed the single life. At least until one night when she laid eyes on the very handsome Kristopher Michaels at her favorite spot Corinthians. She often would go there after a long day at the spa and have a drink or two. She had two very successful spa's one in Baltimore City and one in Baltimore County so she could cater to everyone's needs. Although it was not necessary for her to be there every day Sherry was very hands on and was always at one or the other doing what she did best, making people look and feel beautiful. As successful as she was, she lived a very humbled life.

⚧

One evening as she sat at her favorite table she watched as this six foot tall brother with coco brown skin and black curly hair walk through the front door. She knew at that moment she had to have him if only for one night. She did a little snooping around asking the bartenders and a few regulars about him before she decided to make her move.

Everything she heard about him made her want him even more and the fact that he was married didn't matter to her one bit. She just waited for the perfect opportunity to make her move.

Just like every Friday night Kristopher came in and sat at the bar and ordered his usual shots of Hennessey, but tonight there was something different about him. He seemed troubled and Reds used it to her full advantage. She thought all she wanted was one night of passion, but she was playing for keeps. She wanted Kristopher all to herself and if she had to use the oldest trick in the book to have him, then so be it.

TWO FACE

The moment she sat next to him at the bar her plan was in motion. Whatever it was that had him drinking like a fish she made sure it was the last thing on his mind by the end of the night.

Kristopher was in no condition to drive and she used the opportunity to take him back to her place and seduce him. She knew between the Hennessey and her naked body, a condom would be the last thing on his mind. Although she didn't know his medical history and realized she was putting herself at risk by not using one, she didn't let that stop her. She trusted her gut instinct about the handsome stranger.

"Timing is everything my love and in a couple of months your daddy will know all about you, however I do think it's time for me to take a little trip to Corinthians and see what your daddy is up to," Sherry said as she continued to talk to her unborn child.

Later that week Sherry disguised herself in a long black wig so she wouldn't be recognized by the regulars and especially one in particular. If Kristopher was there she didn't want him to see her until the day she delivered the good news.

She sat patiently in the corner and waited for his arrival and as always at 7:00p.m. sharp he made his appearance. She became moist at the sight of him as flashbacks of their night together entered her mind. She sat and stared at him for what seemed like hours, watching his every move.

As he threw back another shot, Sherry noticed the tan line on his ring finger of his left hand where his wedding ring use to be.

Oh my God, my plan is working better than I thought. I wasn't expecting them to separate until after she heard about the baby, but damn girlfriend must've rolled out. Well, there's only one way to find out.

Sherry rushed towards the front door and bumped right into Kristopher as she fumbled around in her purse looking for her keys.

"I'm sorry Ms. Lady," Kristopher said as he walked by her.

"No, I need to pay attention," Sherry quickly responded.

The sound of her voice made Kristopher stop and look more closely as her voice seemed familiar.

"Damn, he recognized my voice," she said as she walked swiftly out the front door and waited for him to leave.

Kristopher got in his truck and drove home totally unaware that Sherry was following closely behind him. She parked down the street and watched as he entered his beautiful home in Randallstown.

With her hand on her belly she smiled and said, "Now I know just where to find your daddy when it's time to tell him all about you."

Three months later...

⚧

Finally, the moment of truth had arrived and it was time to reveal her soccer ball sized belly to Kristopher.

Sherry wanted to make sure by the time she told Kristopher about the baby that was conceived during their one night of passion it would be too late for an abortion. She wanted her belly to be big enough that she wouldn't have to say a word.

She sat in her vehicle and waited for him to come home. Thirty minutes later Kristopher pulled into the driveway of his home and went inside.

"Ok sweetie it's time to meet your daddy," she said as she slid out of the car and walked slowly to his front door. As she reached the front door her nerves took over and tears begin fill up her eyes as thoughts of rejection crossed her mind.

Ding, Dong, Ding, blared from the doorbell as she pressed it with urgency. When Kristopher opened the door he saw the beautiful woman with flaming red hair standing before him glowing with a big round belly.

TWO FACE

"Hello Kristopher, It's me Reds, the mother of your son," she said with confidence, but fear not far behind.

All Kristopher heard was one word, son. He dropped to his knees, placed his hands on her belly and thanked God for a second chance.

☿

CHAPTER SIX

Diane sat on her deck enjoying the beautiful spring morning with a freshly brewed cup of Joe as she reminisced about the events of the past year. It had been exactly one year since her life had forever changed. She prayed every day that Kristopher would come to his senses so that they could be a family again, which is why she had yet to file for a divorce and to her surprise neither did Kris.

The rumors began to surface about Kristopher having a new family, but Diane prayed it wasn't true. She prayed about it and asked God to reveal it to her if it was.

Later that day Diane decided to take Krisette to the mall to do a little shopping. Krisette was growing like a weed and needed some new clothes for the summer. Although she was not physically born a girl, Krisette was quite beautiful as one.

Mother and daughter walked hand and hand as they went from store to store. As they were making their exit from Macy's Department store they ran right into Kristopher and a beautiful woman pushing a stroller occupied by a bouncing baby boy who looked just like K.J. when he was born six years ago.

It was as if someone pushed the pause button as everyone stood still without saying a word until Krisette looked up and realized it was her father. She was so happy to see him. It had been a whole year since he decided to become an absentee father.

"Daddy," Krisette said as she ran to him with her arms opened wide.

Diane watched, praying that Kristopher would not reject their child once again.

"Hello," Kristopher replied with just a pat on her back.

⚥

Krisette looked up at her father and asked him with tears running down her cheeks, "Daddy why don't you love us anymore?'

Everyone stood there stunned by Krisette's question, but Diane had been pushed to her limit by Kristopher's behavior.

"How dare you treat our child so cold! You couldn't accept the hand that God dealt you so you run out and make a new family!" Diane yelled drawing attention to them.

"Diane, this is not the time or place. You are making a scene," Kristopher responded as he walked over to her and pulled her away from where Sherry was standing with the baby.

Krisette walked over and peeped in the stroller and looked up at Sherry and asked, "Is he my little brother? He looks just like my baby pictures."

"Yes, I guess he is," Sherry replied.

"I hope nothing is wrong with him or my daddy might leave him too," Krisette said before walking over to where her mother stood.

Sherry stood there speechless as she wondered what the hell happened. She knew it was more than an affair that came between them and was determined to find out exactly what it was. After all Kristopher had been nothing but good to her from the moment it was confirmed that Daniel, which was Kristopher's middle name, was indeed his.

As Kristopher walked back over and joined Sherry and his son, Diane followed behind him and took one last look at the adorable baby boy. He shared the same coco brown skin and curly locks as his father. She couldn't help but smile at the innocent child who had nothing to do with this mess he was born into. She walked away and slowly turned back and said, "Kristopher the divorce papers will be in the mail by the end week."

⚥

She took her daughter by the hand and they headed for home. She saw the hurt in her daughter's eyes due to Kris's lack of affection.

"Sweetheart, are you ok?" she asked caressing Krisette's hand.

"I just don't understand why my father doesn't love me anymore and he even had another little boy to replace me."

Diane didn't know how to respond to her daughter's words since she shared the same feelings. They both felt abandoned and betrayed by the man they both loved with all their heart. Diane couldn't help but feel that she was replaced as well. It was like they were no longer good enough for him and didn't fit into what he considered to be a perfect family.

"I hate him and I hope he dies so his new son can grow up without a father too!" Krisette yelled with anger filled eyes.

Once again Diane was shocked by her daughter's words and drove home in silence.

TWO FACE

∞∞∞∞∞

"So are you going to tell me what that was all about?" Sherry asked after they found a quiet spot in the food court.

"That was my wife and...," he paused not knowing what to say.

"Your daughter," Sherry said finishing his sentence.

"Things aren't always as they seem," replied Kristopher.

"What is that supposed to mean Kris?" she asked even more confused than before.

"Krisette was once Kristopher Jr.," Kristopher responded as a single tear fell from his eye.

"What did you say?" asked Sherry with a raised brow. "Did you just say that pretty little girl was your son Kristopher Jr.?"

"Yes, that is exactly what I said."

⚥

"What kind of sick freak is your wife to allow your son to dress up like a girl?" Sherry replied with a slightly raised voice.

"Wait a minute, it's not what you think Sherry," Kristopher said quickly coming to Diane's defense.

"Oh I'm sorry, I didn't mean to upset you by talking about your soon to be ex-wife. I guess you still have some feelings for that sicko."

"I will not allow you to talk about her that way when you don't even know the whole story. Diane is wonderful woman and an awesome mother. She has sacrificed everything for our child and done nothing but give him unconditional love even when I couldn't," Kris said taking a deep breath before telling Sherry what took place.

"Last year KJ. started doing some pretty strange things, well not strange if he was a girl. Diane caught him wearing her makeup and he put on his cousin's princess custom at a Halloween party. We thought maybe he was gay, after all most gay people say they knew at a very young age, but he became depressed and withdrawn so we took him to see a therapist and he diagnosed him as having a gender identity disorder which means he physically looks like a male, but his brain is that of a female."

Sherry sat there with a dropped jaw in complete shock by what she had just heard.

"Wow, I don't know how to respond to that," she said as she stroked his hand.

"I know I am wrong for not standing by my wife and child, but I just couldn't handle it. All I ever wanted was a son and I felt like God had played a cruel joke on me, but now I feel like I have been given a second chance with you and Daniel," he replied as he smiled down at his son.

"Well you have me and Daniel now so just leave all that craziness in the past," she said as she leaned forward and gave her man a kiss.

Little did she know God don't like ugly and ain't too fond of cute.

☿

CHAPTER SEVEN

When it came to her child there was nothing Diane wouldn't do even if it meant killing the man she loved and cherished for fourteen years. After that fateful day in the mall when they ran into Kristopher and his new family, Krisette became depressed and would cry herself to sleep every night. Seeing her child in this much pain was more than she could bear.

Beads of sweat took residence above her top lip as anxiety set in, but nothing would stop her from carrying out her plan of revenge.

"Hello," answered Kris in a slurred voice. It was Friday night and Kristopher was enjoying his usual shots of Hennessey at Corinthians after a long, hard day.

"Hello Kris, as promised I got my lawyer to draw up the divorce papers and I was wondering if you could come by on your way home so we could go over a few things. I would like to make this as informal as possible," Diane said as she fiddled with everything in sight.

"Yeah give me about forty minutes, I wanna get this over with," he replied.

"So do I," Diane said to herself after ending the call.

Forty five minutes later Kris arrived feeling no pain thanks to a few shots of Hennessey.

"I appreciate you coming by," Diane said as she welcomed Kris into her home for the first time. Kristopher was very impressed with Diane's house, but was also wondering how she could afford it. He paid her well in child support, but that still wasn't enough for a place like this. As he looked around she couldn't help, but giggle because he had no idea about her inheritance.

"Where is...?" he asked still unable to refer to his son as his daughter.

"Your daughter is at my sister's house for the weekend," Diane said as she handed him the divorce papers.

"Good, I'm in no mood to deal with that tonight," Kristopher stated as he looked over the documents that would soon end this chapter of his life.

While Kristopher was engrossed in reading the divorce papers, Diane was making him a special cup of coffee. She wasn't making it to wake him up, but to put him to sleep. She spiked it with liquid Benadryl. Whenever Kris's allergies were out of control he would take it and it would put him out for the rest of the night. This time she hoped it would be more permanent.

"Kris, I made you a cup of iced coffee to sober you up for your drive home. Black and strong just the way you like it," Diane said as she handed him the deadly cup of Joe.

"Thanks, I always loved your coffee," he said while slurping it down. Diane enjoyed watching him drink every drop of her sweet revenge.

"I hope you find everything to be fair. You can have your lawyer go over them and here is my lawyers card so he can reach him if either of you have any questions or concerns."

Diane could see that the Benadryl was already taking effect so it was time to get him out of there. "You better get home before your girlfriend sends out the National Guard," she said.

"Yeah, I need to get home to my family." His words pierced Diane's heart and left her with no regrets. She practically pushed him out the door and into his vehicle.

"Drive safely," Diane said with a devilish grin.

Kris rolled down the window hoping the night air would wake him up, but four shots of Hennessey,

⚨

a Corona and a double dose of Benadryl made for a deadly combination.

As he headed West on I695 headed for his home in Randallstown his driving became more reckless by the minute. The drivers around him frantically tried to escape his path as he dodged in and out of traffic.

No longer able to keep his eyes open Kristopher's car drifted to the right causing his truck to bounce off the concrete barrier right back into traffic where he was hit dead on by a tractor trailer and was killed instantly.

∞∞∞∞∞∞

It was getting late and Sherry found herself in the same predicament as Diane just one year ago.

Now she was the one sitting home worried and wondering where Kris was and why he wasn't answering his cell phone. She decided to turn on the TV to take her mind off things. She watched the news as they were reporting a fatal accident on I695. As she looked a little closer she realized that one of the mangled vehicles was Kris's black Ford Expedition. She picked her the phone and frantically dialed his cell praying to God that her eyes were deceiving her. As the phone rang and rang, she screamed in horror at the thought of losing Kris. She went to Daniel's bedroom and picked her son up and held him tight as tears poured from her eyes. It broke her heart to know that her precious baby boy would grow up without his father.

∞∞∞∞∞∞

Ding Dong Ding blared from the doorbell once again as officers arrived to deliver the bad news to Diane.

"Yes. Can I help you officers?" Diane asked wearing a confused look on her face,

"Sorry to bother you at such a late hour, but are you Mrs. Michaels, wife of Kristopher Michaels?" asked the officer.

"Yes, I am."

"I'm afraid I have some bad news. Your husband Kristopher was involved in a fatal accident this evening on I695 and he was killed on impact," the officer explained.

Diane grabbed her chest and allowed some tears to fall freely as her act of revenge was complete.

"Oh my God, he just left here a little while ago and I tried to sober him up with some coffee, but I guess it wasn't enough."

"Are you and your husband having problems? I noticed there were two addresses listed for you as his emergency contact."

"Actually Officer, he came by to go over the divorce papers before turning them over to his lawyer. We have been separated for a year now and he has a new family."

"Oh I see, well he still had you listed as his person to contact. Is there anyone else we should notify?"

TWO FACE

"I appreciate that, but I will let everyone know. That knock on the door can be quite unsettling," Diane replied with another agenda in mind.

"Well I'm sorry for your loss Mrs. Michaels," the officer said before returning to his vehicle.

"I will be more than happy to deliver the bad news to that redheaded bitch," Diane said to herself as she closed the door behind the officer.

∞∞∞∞∞∞

Sherry waited all night for someone to confirm her worst fears that Kristopher was indeed dead, but not a phone call or the dreaded knock on the door was received.

Early the next morning Diane showed up dressed in all black knocking on the door of the home she was once shared with Kristopher.

"Diane, what are you doing here?" asked Sherry with blood shot eyes.

☿

"I gather by your blood shot eyes that you already know that our beloved Kristopher was killed in a fatal accident last night on I695," Diane blurted out with no remorse.

"I saw it on the news, but was praying it wasn't him," Sherry responded with her eyes filled with tears.

"What a horrible way to find out that the father of your son is dead. If only Kris would have handled his business you my dear would not be in this mess you're in now."

"What do you mean handled his business?" Sherry asked with an attitude.

"You see dear, not only did Kris forget to change his emergency contact, he never added you and your bastard son to his will. Therefore I get everything including this house and you have exactly one week to get the hell out of my house," Diane shouted and turned and walked away.

"You fucking liar, Kris would never do that to me and his son," Sherry yelled back as she fell to her knees and cried.

Diane turned to her and yelled, "Karma's a bitch!"

CHAPTER EIGHT

It had been five years since the tragic death of Kristopher Michaels. The crash was ruled an accident due to the amount of alcohol and Benadryl found in his system as well as witness statements that confirmed that they saw Kristopher falling asleep at the wheel.

Some might say Diane got away with murder, but like she told Sherry, "Karma's a bitch." two years after Kristopher's death Diane found a lump in her breast during a self-exam and immediately went to her doctor who after testing confirmed she had a malignant tumor in her right breast. Diane was now fighting the same battle her mother did so many years ago. After getting both breasts removed and replaced with implants as well as undergoing treatment, Diane was now in remission. She never thought of it as her punishment for what she did to Kristopher, but her fate. She and her sister both knew the odds of one if not both of them getting it because of their family history.

Krisette was now eleven years old, almost the same age Diane was when her mother lost her battle with breast cancer. The thought of losing her mother devastated Krisette, after all her mother was all she had. Her mother loved her for who she was and not once tried to make her be that little boy her husband longed for.

When Diane told Krisette that her father was killed in a car accident, she looked her mother in the eyes and said, "That was God's way of punishing him for abandoning his family and if I couldn't have a father, baby Daniel couldn't either."

Even after what she had done, seeing the coldness in her daughter's eyes when she spoke about her father scared Diane. She prayed that

Krisette's monthly therapy sessions with Dr. Stevenson would one day heal her broken heart.

Krisette was now undergoing physical evaluations as well so she could begin taking hormone therapy which had to begin before she reached puberty. They had to be absolutely sure that this was not just some phase Krisette was going through, but after being evaluated both mentally and physically Krisette was well on her way to becoming a beautiful little girl both inside and out.

The day had finally arrived for Krisette to meet with the endocrinologist who would be assisting her with the hormone therapy. Krisette anxiously waited for the doctor to enter the exam room.

"Hello Krisette and Mrs. Michaels," the doctor said upon entering the room.

"Hello Dr. Ghee," they spoke in unison.

"So how are you feeling today sweetie?" the pretty petite doctor asked.

TWO FACE

"I'm excited Dr. Ghee," Krisette answered smiling from ear to ear.

"Ok, well I won't keep you waiting much longer, but let me explain the effects that the hormone therapy will have on your body. The Anti-Androgen will block the male hormones that your body naturally produces and after taking the Estrogen along with the anti-androgen you will notice your skin will become softer, you will eventually develop breasts; you will see a decrease in the size of your penis and testicles, there will be a redistribution of body fat and increased body fat which will mean the hips, thighs and buttocks will collect the majority of this distribution while the redistribution will result in a smaller waistline. Your body will experience many changes. You may notice some changes within months, but most will be gradual. I promise you will not wake up tomorrow with a big behind and breasts," explained Dr. Ghee. They all laughed. "There are also some side effects that I need to mention and they can be very serious. The side effects of using these drugs are heart disease, stroke, breast or testicular cancer, blood clots, liver disease."

"Dr. Ghee, none of that matters to me, if I have to live with this body I would rather die anyway," Krisette interrupted with a serious stare.

"Ok sweetie, I understand, but it's my job to inform you about the good, the bad and the ugly. What you are about to do is very serious and will affect the rest of your life."

"Krisette, are you absolutely sure this is what you want to do?" Diane asked with concern as she cupped her daughter's chin.

"Mom, as I said before, I would rather die than to live this way," replied Krisette.

"So if you are ready, we can begin."

"I've been ready since the day I was five years old," Krisette replied anxiously.

"Ok first I will administer the Estradiol, which is the estrogen and it has the feminizing effects such as the softening of the skin, nipple and breast development, decrease the size of your testicles, it will decrease any muscle mass and increase body fat and you will have fewer morning erections. I will be giving you a shot in the muscle of your arm once every four weeks. Now for anti-androgens, I am prescribing 2.5 mg of Proscar. You are to take 1 pill every other day. As I said before this will block the effects of testosterone, meaning it will reduce the male physical traits."

Krisette was becoming impatient as Dr. Ghee carefully explained not once, but twice the effects of each drug to Diane and Krisette.

"Before I give you your first injection do either of you have any questions?"

"No," they both said.

"Ok roll up your sleeve," Dr. Ghee requested as she put on her gloves. She then wiped the area where the injection would be given with an alcohol pad, she filled the syringe with the Estradiol and slowly injected the muscle of Krisette's right arm.

"You may feel some soreness around the injection site for a couple of days or even some nausea, headaches, or vomiting may occur. Mrs. Michaels, if you have any questions or concerns, please don't hesitate to call me. Be sure to stop by the front desk to make your four week appointment for your next injection and I will also be doing some blood work to check your hormone levels and to keep eye on your liver. It's been my pleasure," Dr. Ghee said as she shook Diane's hand.

"Thank you so much doctor. You have made my daughter so happy and when she's happy I'm happy."

Dr. Ghee smiled and was stunned when Krisette leapt off the exam table into her arms.

"Thank you Dr. Ghee," Krisette said with tears in her eyes. Krisette knew this was just the beginning of her long road to womanhood. There would be many more bumps along the way, but finally her physical transformation was well underway.

CHAPTER NINE

After years of being trapped in a body that wasn't compatible to her mind, Krisette was finally finding peace as the two were beginning to harmonize.

Krisette smiled as she admired her newly developing body in the full length mirror attached to the outside of the bathroom door. She couldn't believe the changes in her body after only six months of hormone therapy.

Her coco brown skin was as smooth as silk, her bust blossomed into a perfect 32B followed by a slender waistline that accentuated her apple shaped behind and ended with her long shapely legs. She was becoming a beautiful combination of both her parents with her father's curly locks, big brown eyes and coco brown skin combined with her mother's hour glass figure.

"Wow," Krisette said in amazement posing as if she were having a photo shoot. The hormone therapy changed more than her body, it gave Krisette a new attitude.

Diane quietly watched from down the hall and saw something she had never seen before, Krisette was happy and beaming with confidence. Diane's eyes filled with tears at the beautiful sight before her. Her emotions became uncontrollable and her presence was revealed.

"Mom, are you spying on me?" Krisette asked.

"I'm sorry baby," Diane replied.

"Why are you crying?" she asked wiping her mother's tears away.

"Do you know how long I have waited for his moment? All I ever wanted was to see you happy. Your happiness means more to me than my own, "Diane replied.

"I am happy mom, I finally feel free and it's all because of you."

"Sweetheart I only did what any parent would do."

"You could have turned your back on me like daddy, but instead you sacrificed everything for me. You accepted me for who I am and not what you wanted me to be," Krisette responded with a warm embrace.

"Krisette, the love between a mother and her child is like no other and there is nothing I wouldn't do for you."

Krisette could feel every word her mother spoke and knew it to be true.

"Mom I have been doing a lot of thinking and was wondering if I could go to a public high school. I want to live as a normal teenage girl and besides I don't want to miss prom and graduation."

"I understand sweetheart, I just don't want a repeat of what happen in elementary school."

"Look at me mom, no one will know," Krisette said with confidence.

⚥

As much as Diane didn't like the idea of Krisette going to a public school, she agreed to it. After all the progress Krisette was making, she didn't want to do anything to hinder her daughter's progress.

From the looks of her no one would ever believe she was born a male, but the thought of Krisette going to a public high school made Diane extremely nervous after the incident that took place back when Krisette attempted to go to elementary school.

"Sweetheart, if you need me just called me and I will be right here to pick you up," Diane said as Krisette exited the car.

"Thanks mom, but I will be fine. Stop worrying so much," Krisette replied. Telling Diane not to worry was like telling her not to breath.

TWO FACE

Krisette was very excited about her first day at Severna Park High School. She walked the halls with confidence and was not at all uncomfortable with the stares she was receiving. In fact she liked it, however this was the first time she got the attention of boys and wasn't sure how to respond to it.

She caught the boys making comments about her figure and this only boosted her confidence even more. She walked with her head held high and an extra sway in her hips.

"Hey cutie, what's your name?" asked a tall thin young man.

"Krisette," replied with a smile. Just as the young man approached Krisette, another young lady grabbed her by the arm pulling her away.

"Excuse me, he was just saying hello," Krisette said snatching away from the young lady.

"Girl, I just saved you and you will thank me later. That's Corey Thompson, the biggest freak in the school. All he wants is to get in your panties and tell everybody about it. Of course he comes out smelling like a rose while you look like a hoe," she said.

"Well in that case I will thank you now...I'm sorry, what is your name?" Krisette asked.

"My name is Lauren and I believe I heard you say your name is Krisette," said Lauren.

"Yes I did," Krisette said to her new friend.

Later that day, Diane paced back and forth waiting for Krisette to come through the front door with stories of her first day of school. She assumed all was well since she never received a phone call. Krisette finally entered the house with a bland look on her face, leaving Diane standing there searching her face for some type of expression.

"Well honey how was your first day of high school?" she asked.

Finally Krisette smiled widely and said, "It was great mom. I met this really nice girl named Lauren who happens to be in all my classes and I even got hit on by a boy."

"What did he say to you? Were you scared? How did you feel about that?" Diane asked not giving Krisette a chance to answer one question before asking another.

"Slow down mom," Krisette said as they both laughed. "He said hello and asked me my name, but that's when Lauren showed up and saved me from the biggest playboy in the school. She said he tries to get in all the girls panties and then talks about them. Well he would definitely be in for the shock of his life if he tried to get into mine," Krisette explained making light of her situation.

Diane couldn't help but laugh at her daughter's remark. "I'm glad you had a good first day. My stomach was in knots all day, but sweetie how did you feel when the boy approached you?'

"Actually mom it made me feel good about myself. I figured if a boy is showing interest in me then I must really look like a girl. Like I told you mom, you have nothing to worry about. No one will ever know; it's our little secret."

⚥

Things were going very well at school and Diane had never seen Krisette so happy. She was thriving in all her classes and had made many new friends along the way. Over the next year, Krisette became very close with Lauren who showed her the ropes of her new environment. Lauren's birthday had arrived and she was celebrating with a sleepover. Now that they were best friends, Lauren begged Krisette to come. Krisette always made up an excuse not to attend all the others, but Lauren wasn't taking no for an answer this time.

She knew her mother wasn't going to be happy about it, but she didn't want it to come between her and Lauren's friendship.

"Hello Sweetheart, how was your day?" Diane asked as Krisette walked through the front door.

"It was okay," Krisette replied dreading the conversation that was about to take place.

"What's wrong? Did something happen at school today?" she asked with concern.

"No, nothing like that. Lauren is having a sleep over this weekend for her birthday and she really wants me to come."

"Krisette, it's not that I don't want you to have fun with your friends, but you have to be careful considering your situation and that little problem you've been having."

"I know mom, but I don't want Lauren to get mad at me. Every time she invites me to one of her sleepovers I don't show up and this is her birthday. Please mom, can I go?"

Diane looked into those big brown eyes and gave in. "Ok Krisette, but please be mindful of your situation."

"You're the best mom," Krisette said before kissing Diane on the cheek.

∞∞∞∞∞∞

It was Friday night and all of Lauren's closet friends were gathered at her house for her birthday sleep over. They watched movies, played board games, ate junk food until their bellies ached and Lauren's mom even had someone come in to give the girls manicures and pedicures. A good time was being had by all, especially Krisette who seemed to be having more fun than everyone including the birthday girl. Krisette was happy and finally felt like she was one of the girls, at least until morning came.

As Lauren tried carefully to get out of the bed without waking Krisette, she noticed the sheets were lifted up like an Indian tepee. She snatched the sheet off of Krisette to see what she was hiding under the sheets and it wasn't at all what she expected.

"What the fuck?" Lauren yelled waking up the other girls.

Krisette immediately jumps up from a sound sleep and ran into the bathroom with the sheet wrapped around her.

"Get out of there, you sick freak!" Lauren yelled.

The other girls just laid there still half asleep wondering what had happen for Lauren to call Krisette a sick freak.

Meanwhile Krisette was in the bathroom filled with sadness and humiliation trying to figure out how to get out of there without facing Lauren. She decided to make a run for it and leave everything behind, even the best friend she ever had.

She snatched the door open and knocked down everything in sight including Lauren and made her way to the front door. She didn't stop running until she made it home which fortunately was only five blocks away.

When she got home she banged on the front door until she heard Diane turning the locks. As soon as Diane opened the door she fell to the ground and wept in her mother's arms. She didn't have to say a word Diane already knew what happened and wondered how Krisette would recover from this.

⚥

CHAPTER TEN

After the incident at Lauren's house Krisette became withdrawn and depressed. She stayed locked up in her room all day and night. Some of her friends from school were calling, but she wouldn't talk to anyone, including her mother. Diane tried her best to comfort her daughter, but there was nothing she could do or say that would ease the pain or humiliation she felt.

"Krisette, I made you some crab soup!" Diane yelled from the bottom of the stairs. Diane knew how much she loved her crab soup and was hoping she loved it enough to get her out of her room.

TWO FACE

When Krisette didn't answered Diane decided to go check on her. "Krisette," Diane said as she gently knocked on the door and still received no response.

"Krisette," she said in a nervous tone as she slowly opened the door to her daughter's bedroom.

"Oh my God, Krisette," Diane screamed after finding her daughter laying unconscious next to her bed with both her wrists slit. She checked for a pulse and it was weak, but present. She ran to the phone and dialed 911 as she returned to her daughter's side.

"Please God, don't take by baby!"

"911, what is the state of your emergency?" asked the 911 operator in a calm voice.

"Please help me, I just found my daughter unconscious with both her wrists slit. She has a pulse, but it is very weak."

"What is your location?'

"4552 Lovestream Ct."

"Okay, try to remain calm, help is on the way, in the meantime apply pressure to your daughter's wrists until the ambulance arrives. That will help slow down the bleeding," said the 911 operator.

Minutes later the ambulance arrived and rushed Krisette to the nearest hospital.

While Krisette was being cared for by the doctors and nurses Diane made a call to Dr. Stevenson who had been working with Krisette since she was five years old. He was shocked to hear of Krisette's suicide attempt because she had been so happy after receiving the hormone therapy two years ago. He agreed it would be best for her to talk to someone familiar rather than a total stranger who might not have experience with transgender children.

"Mrs. Michaels, you may see you daughter now. She is all stitched up and a little groggy from the pain meds, but physically she will be fine. I would like her to stay a couple of days for observation and have her talk to our psychiatrist. She is very lucky, you found her just in time," stated the doctor.

TWO FACE

"Thank you so much doctor, but I already called her therapist and he is on the way," Diane said with her hand extended.

Diane quietly entered the room trying not to wake Krisette from what looked like a peaceful sleep, but suddenly she cried out and tears poured from her eyes.

"Sweetheart, mommy is right here," Diane said as she stoked her daughter's curly locks.

Krisette slowly opened her eyes and wept even harder when she saw her mother's face. Diane wiped her tears away and kissed her gently on the forehead.

"Don't cry baby girl, everything will be ok."

"I'm so sorry mom, if I would have listened to you in the first place none of this would have happened," Krisette cried.

"Let's put that behind us and think about the future," Diane replied.

⚧

"What future? I don't want to live another day like this. I'm tired of people calling me names. I'm tired of not being accepted for who I am. My own father couldn't accept me so why do I think others will. You should have let me die!" Krisette yelled.

Krisette's words pierced Diane's heart and she knew she had to do something or she would lose her daughter.

"Krisette, don't say..."

Before Diane could finish her sentence Dr. Stevenson entered the room.

"Diane let me talk to Krisette alone for a moment please," Dr. Stevenson requested.

"Okay, Krisette I will be right outside your door."

"Krisette the last time we spoke you were so happy with the results of your hormone therapy, everything at school was going well. What happened to bring this on?" Dr. Stevenson asked.

"Everything was great and I finally felt like a normal teenage girl, until I went to my best friend's sleep over and woke up with a hard on," Krisette replied with tears streaming down her face.

"So I gather someone noticed it then?"

"Noticed it, she screamed so loud she woke up the whole house."

"I'm sorry to hear that Krisette. I'm sure that was very embarrassing for you, but let me ask you this. If you consider this young lady your best friend, why didn't you confide in her about your condition?"

"The outcome would have been the same, so it doesn't matter."

"You don't know that Krisette. I bet she is more upset with that fact that you didn't tell her. You have to be honest with people who are important to you and let them decide if they can handle it or not and if not than you aren't as important to them as they are to you. Think about what I said and I will be back tomorrow. You get some rest kiddo," Dr. Stevenson said as he exited the room.

☿

Krisette laid there and wondered if Lauren would have reacted any different if she would have told her the truth.

"How are you feeling? Did you have a nice talk with Dr. Stevenson?" Diane asked as she entered the room just as Dr. Stevenson was leaving.

"I'm okay."

Diane wasn't sure what Dr. Stevenson said to her daughter, but Krisette was much calmer than before.

"I'm glad you like Dr. Stevenson and you are able to talk openly with him."

"He understood me when no one else did. There may be some truth to what he said, but it didn't change how I feel. I need to have the sex reassignment surgery as soon as possible and by any means necessary," Krisette replied.

Diane knew by the look in her daughter's eyes that this was a life or death situation and she had to do whatever it took it make this happen.

"Krisette, you must be eighteen years old to have the surgery done," Diane explained.

"You might as well start planning my funeral because I refuse to wait four and a half years to have it done. Mom I'm sorry, but I can't. I just can't do it," Krisette sobbed. Diane held her close and whispered, "Don't worry sweetheart, like I told you before I would do anything for you."

Diane couldn't take the chance of losing her daughter even if it meant walking through the gates of hell to make Krisette happy. She knew she would have to find the best cosmetic surgeon in the field that was willing to break the rules for the right price. After all money was not a problem, she still had some of her inheritance as well as the money from Kristopher's insurance policies.

⚥

CHAPTER ELEVEN

A couple of days passed and Krisette was discharged from the hospital. After Diane got her settled in her room she jumped on the computer in search of the best cosmetic surgeon in sex reassignment.

After only a few hours Diane was pleasantly surprised to find a surgeon right there in Maryland at Mercy Medical Center, a Dr. Robert Thompson Jr. After looking over his credentials and visiting his website, which included before and after pictures of his work, Diane was very impressed. However none of it would matter if he declined her offer. She picked up the phone and scheduled a consultation for the following Monday, which would allow her time to make a trip to the bank.

TWO FACE

Diane decided not to tell Krisette anything until Dr. Thompson agreed to do the surgery. The last thing she wanted to do was raise her hopes only to disappoint her again.

∞∞∞∞∞∞

Diane arrived promptly at Dr. Thompson's Office at 9 a.m. on Monday. She was his first patient of the day and waited patiently to be seen while butterflies danced around in her stomach. She knew what she was doing was wrong, but her daughter happiness was well worth the risk.

"Mrs. Michaels," said the very attractive receptionist breaking her trance.

Wow, I wonder what she has had done. She is stunning, Diane thought to herself as she walked in Dr. Thompson's office.

"Hello Mrs. Michaels, I'm Dr. Thompson," he said extending his hand.

"Hello," Diane replied as they shook hands.

There was an instant attraction between the two of them that was obvious to them both.

"What brings you here today? I hope not to have a sex reassignment because that would be such an injustice," Dr. Thompson flirted.

Diane blushed and replied, "No, I'm very happy with who and what I am."

"As you should be, so how can I help you?"

"I'm here about my daughter Krisette, who was born Kristopher, but since the age of five he has insisted that he is a girl trapped in a boy's body. We took him to go see Dr. Stevenson and he confirmed that he had a gender identity disorder.

"Would that be Dr. Paul Stevenson in Owings Mills?" asked Dr. Thompson.

"Yes it is," Diane replied with enthusiasm. She prayed that this would help and not hurt his decision.

"He is an excellent therapist and has referred a lot of patients to me. Did he refer you as well?"

"No he didn't, I did a little research of my own and it led me right to you," Diane responded in a flirtatious tone.

I never thought I would put cream in my coffee, but Dr. Thompson was gorgeous, Diane thought to herself. He stood a little over six feet tall with an athletic build, smooth vanilla skin, and piercing blue eyes.

"Ok, so where is your son or should I say your daughter?" he asked curiously.

"She doesn't know I'm here. I didn't want her to be disappointed if you decided not to do her surgery."

"My schedule is a little full, but as long as she meets the criteria I see no reason why I wouldn't unless there's something you're not telling me," he replied.

"Dr. Thompson let me be straight with you my daughter is only thirteen and I am perfectly aware that you have to be between the ages of eighteen and twenty one years old to have this surgery done, but

I'm willing to do anything to make my daughter happy.

Although she has lived as a girl since her diagnosis, she is miserable. She has been teased, beaten and constantly rejected, even by her own father. A few days ago she attempted suicide and she told me she would rather die than to live this way. Please Dr. Thompson, I'm begging you, please help my daughter." Diane pleaded with streams of tears coming from her eyes.

This story had become all too familiar as he hears from his patients on a daily basis the pain and rejection they endure from their family, friends and society.

"Mrs. Michaels, I'm sorry, but Krisette doesn't meet the criteria for the sex reassignment surgery. I'm afraid my hands are tied," Dr. Thompson replied.

Diane grabbed the black leather briefcase that rested on the floor next to her and walked over and carefully placed it on his beautiful cherry wood desk.

TWO FACE

"Will this untie your hands?" Diane asked as she opened the briefcase filled with stacks of money.

Dr. Thompson looked in total shock at the stacks of money that lay before him, not because he had never seen it before, but it was certainly the first time someone tried to pay him to bend the rules.

"Mrs. Michaels, I....." She placed her index finger across his lips and whispered in a seductive tone, "I will do anything for my daughter."

He saw the desperation in her eyes and decided to take full advantage of the situation. "Mrs. Michaels, please don't insult me with your money. I am one of the top cosmetic surgeons in the country; I don't need or want your money. I want you," he stated very cocky.

Diane couldn't believe what she had just heard. She walked over to him and slapped him across his face, but that seemed to excite him even more. He grabbed her arms and held them behind her back as he kissed her with a passion she never

☿

knew existed. At first she put up a struggle trying to set herself free, but soon gave in to her desires within.

"Stop, I can't do this," Diane said as she pulled away.

"I thought you said you would do anything for your daughter and I know you want me just as much as I want you," he replied as he planted small kisses on her neck.

"I meant I can't do it here, not now," she said returning his kisses.

Her response stopped him dead in his tracks. "So come back around five, I should be done by then," he said anxiously.

"Ok doc, I will see you at five." She gathered her things and gave him one last kiss before leaving his office. As she was closing the door behind her she noticed the receptionist sitting at her desk.

"Michelle is it?" Diane asked with a smile.

"Yes it is Mrs. Michaels; can I help you with something?" Michelle asked politely.

"You most certainly can. Is it possible for you to step away from your desk for a moment so we can have a little more privacy," Diane replied.

"Yes, I will tell Dr. Thompson I'm going to the ladies room."

"Ok I will meet you there, where is it?"

"It's down the hall on the right," instructed Michelle.

Diane made her way to the restroom and waited patiently for Michelle to join her. She needed some insurance just in case Dr. Thompson got what he wanted and then refused to do the surgery.

"What can I do for you Mrs. Michaels?" Michelle asked as she locked the door to the ladies room so they wouldn't be interrupted.

"How loyal are you to Dr. Thompson?"

"Dr. Thompson saved my life. He was there for me when everyone turned their back on me. He took me off the street, gave me a place to stay, a job and he did my sex reassignment surgery free of charge," explained Michelle,

Diane couldn't believe her eyes; this stunning young woman was once a man. Michelle was a curvy petite young woman with a golden brown complexion, long straight honey blonde hair that stopped in the middle of her back, green eyes and high cheek bones.

"Oh my God, Michelle you use to be a man?" Diane asked covering her mouth in disbelief. She looked Michelle up and down and from side to side.

"Yes, I was born Michael King."

"I must say you are a gorgeous young lady. I have to do whatever it takes for Dr. Thompson to do this surgery which brings me to why I asked you in here. My daughter Krisette was also born a male but desperately wants to become a woman, but she is too young to have the surgery. I offered Dr. Thompson twenty thousand dollars to bend the rules and he refused the money, but wants me instead.

Michelle didn't bat an eye at what she was being told. Dr. Thompson was a real ladies man who always got what he wanted.

"So what is it you need from me?" asked Michelle.

"I am meeting him here at five to give him a down payment for my daughter's surgery and I need some insurance just in case he tries to back out."

"What kind of insurance Mrs. Michaels?"

"I need you to film us having sex in his office."

"Oh I don't know if I can do that?" Michelle replied walking towards the door.

"Not even for five thousand dollars." Diane said with cash in hand."

Michelle stood there with a raised brow and a devilish grin spread across her face.

"Ok I will do it, but I pray I don't lose my job over this."

"Michelle, don't worry your pretty little head about this. He won't even notice you and besides I'll give you a copy of the tape so you will always have some insurance of your own. I will have the camera ready for you when I arrive later this evening."

"Ok, I need to get back now. I'm sure he is wondering where I am by now, Michelle said as she wrapped the money in paper towels and headed back to her desk.

∞∞∞∞∞∞

Later that evening Diane arrived back at Dr. Thompson office wearing a black trench coat and black Louis Vuitton pumps. She got there a few minutes early so she could give Michelle the camera and a few instructions.

"Don't worry sweetie he will be too deep in my pussy to notice you filming us. Just make sure you get a clear shot of his face," Diane whispered before knocking on the door.

"Come in."

TWO FACE

When Diane entered the room Dr. Thompson's face lit up with excitement. As she slowly walked over to his desk she unbuttoned the trench coat and revealed her nakedness that was hidden underneath. She made herself comfortable on top of his desk directly in front of him. He inhaled her sweetness and buried his head between her thighs and enjoyed the feast before him.

Just as she was about to cum, he stood up and freed his throbbing manhood and secured it with a condom. He entered her slowly as he sucked her right nipple.

"Oh yes," Diane screamed with delight.

"You like that baby."

As things got hot and heavy been the two of them, Michelle managed to sneak in and film the sex session that was taking place without being discovered.

After almost an hour of sexing Diane on just about every piece of furniture in the office, he finally collapsed on Diane's chest.

⚥

"That was everything I thought it would be and more," he whispered.

"So does this mean you will do my daughter's surgery?" Diane asked getting straight to the point.

"Yes, call Michelle tomorrow and set up an appointment so that the three of us can sit down and discuss the SRS."

"Thank you so much Dr. Thompson you have no idea how much this means to me, "Diane cried.

"I think I have some idea and that's Dr. Feel Good," he replied. They both laughed and shared a kiss.

CHAPTER TWELVE

The next day Diane called Michelle to schedule the meeting between Dr. Thompson, Krisette and herself to discuss the details of the sex reassignment surgery and invited Michelle to lunch so she could check out the sex tape that was made the night before. Although she didn't think it was needed, it's always good to have insurance.

"Wow Michelle, you did a great job and I appreciate it. I know it was hard given everything he has done for you. Here's an extra thousand dollars, treat yourself to something special, you deserve it," Diane said after watching the tape.

"Thank you so much Mrs. Michaels, but I have walked in your daughter's shoes and I know exactly what she's going through. I'm looking forward to meeting her tomorrow," Michelle replied.

"I'm looking forward to it as well. I decided to surprise her; she has no idea about the appointment tomorrow. Well sweetie you have a great day and if you ever need anything don't hesitate to call," Diane said as they embraced and parted ways.

∞∞∞∞∞∞

"Krisette it's time to get out this bed and join the land of the living. You have been in the room long enough and the pity party ends today!" Diane yelled as she opened the blinds allowing the light of the sun to dance across her daughter's face.

"Mommy, close the blinds," Krisette replied pulling the sheet over her face.

Diane snatched the sheet off of her face and yelled, "Krisette I know you have been through a lot, but you haven't been alone in this. I have been right there with you and I have done everything in my power to make you happy so all I'm asking is for you to get your ass out this bed and get dressed because I'm getting you out this house if it's the last thing I do!" Diane yelled with tear filled eyes.

It broke Krisette's heart to see her mother cry and she knew everything her mother said was true. She has been fighting this battle with her since day one. So she dragged herself out of bed and made her way into the bathroom to shower.

Diane eagerly waited for Krisette to come downstairs so they could be on the way to Dr. Thompson's office. She could not wait to see the look on her face when she finds out that she can have the sex reassignment surgery after all.

"I'm ready," Krisette said forcing herself to smile.

"I promise you my love, it's going to be a great day," Diane said as she caressed her daughter's cheek. The appointment wasn't until noon so Diane took Krisette out to breakfast and did some browsing at The Gallery in the Inner Harbor before heading over to Mercy Medical Center to meet with Dr. Thompson.

When they arrived at Mercy Medical Center and walked into the Center for Plastic and Reconstructive Surgery Department Krisette's face lit up like it was Christmas morning.

"Mom you did it, you found somebody to do my surgery?" Krisette was overwhelmed with emotion. She couldn't believe that her dream was finally coming true.

"Krisette I would like you to meet a very special young lady, Michelle. Michelle this is my daughter Krisette."

"Hello Krisette, I've heard a lot about you and I'm very pleased to meet you," said Michelle.

"It's nice to meet you too Michelle," Krisette said as they shook hands.

"Sweetheart, you and Michelle have a lot in common," stated Diane.

"Really?" asked Krisette with a confused stare.

"Yes we do Krisette. I was born Michael King," replied Michelle.

"Wow, you look amazing," said Krisette.

"You are in excellent hands with Dr. Thompson," Michelle responded as she noticed him patiently waiting.

"Hello ladies, Mrs. Michaels and Krisette if you would join me in my office we can get started," said Dr. Thompson.

"Good morning Dr. Thompson, this is Krisette. As I told you she was diagnosed with gender identity disorder at the age of five and has been living as a female ever since and she started hormone therapy two years ago," Diane explained.

"I must say you look great Krisette. You definitely meet the criteria with the exception of your age, but since we already have your mom's permission we can move forward with the SRS which stands for sex reassignment surgery. There are a few things we need to discuss about the surgery such as cost, pre-op, side effects, after care, your recovery and things of that nature, but before I get into the details I need to know that you are absolutely sure you are ready to do this?"

"Dr. Thompson, I am absolutely ready to become the woman I was meant to be," Krisette replied.

"Ok that's great, but did your mom explain to you that I have a very busy schedule and it will be a few months before I can get you in," he explained.

"Can we do it on my birthday, May 22nd?"

"Actually that would be perfect. Now I'm going to go over a few things as I said before and then have you and your mom watch a video of the actual surgery being done. It just makes it easier to understand instead of me trying to explain it."

"The cost of the surgery will be about thirty five thousand dollars that includes the consultation, my doctor's fee, your hospital stay, anesthesia and aftercare. The surgery lasts about three hours and you should expect to stay in the hospital for about five days or more if we run into any problems. Now the video is very graphic, but you will see exactly what will be done as well as the final results, it will also go over the risks and complications, side effects and how to care for yourself after the surgery. If you have any questions after the video please don't be afraid to ask."

Dr. Thompson put in the video and Diane and Krisette watched intensely without batting an eye. When the video ended Dr. Thompson asked Krisette once again, "Krisette after watching the video, are you sure you want to do this?"

"I am positive Dr. Thompson," she answered with confidence.

"Ok, I just want to be sure. Mrs. Michaels you can tell Michelle to schedule the surgery for May 22nd and give her your insurance information and if you are paying cash I will need half now and the balance must be paid a week before the surgery. If you don't have any questions, you have a great day and I will be in touch," Dr. Thompson stated as he walked them to the door.

Krisette gave Dr. Thompson a big hug and said, "Thank you so much Dr. Thompson, you just saved my life."

CHAPTER THIRTEEN

May 22nd, arrived and just as Kristopher Michaels Jr. was born fourteen years ago, Krisette thought it would only be appropriate for her to have her sex reassignment surgery on this day as well. After years of fighting between her mind and her body, today she would be made whole. Today will be the first day of the rest of her life.

"Happy birthday sweetheart!" Diane yelled upon entering Krisette's bedroom.

"Thanks mom."

"Are you ready for your big day?" Diane asked smiling.

⚥

"I have been waiting for this day for so long and now I can finally be the girl I was supposed to be."

"Well we don't want to be late so let's get going," Diane said as she helped Krisette with her bags.

The ride to the hospital was quiet as they both reminisced on everything they had been through. All the rejection from family and friends, but none hurt as much as the rejection from her father. Krisette often wondered why he couldn't accept her as his child no matter what gender she was, but none of that mattered anymore. Today she will become a female in every sense of the word and she would never have to worry about being accepted or rejected by anyone ever again.

∞∞∞∞∞∞

Krisette was prepped and ready to go, but there was one thing left to do. Diane and Krisette held hands and prayed.

TWO FACE

"Dear God, I know you don't make mistakes and we are in no way trying to do your job, but merely trying to correct a wrong. Please God watch over my baby and guide Dr. Thompson's hands as he performs this surgery that will make my child whole again. In Jesus name I pray, Amen."

∞∞∞∞∞∞

Three hours seemed more like three days to Diane as she paced back and forth anxiously waiting to hear some news about Krisette's condition. She stopped dead in her tracks when she saw the recovery room doors swing open and Dr. Thompson walking towards her.

"Everything went as expected and she is doing just fine. As soon as she wakes up they will be transporting her to her room and we have it all set up so you can stay right by her side," Dr. Thompson explained.

"Thank you so much Dr. Thompson," Diane replied with a warm embrace.

⚥

"You are welcome Mrs. Michaels. She will be closely monitored by the nurse as well as myself and given instructions on her aftercare. It shouldn't be much longer so you can get the room number from the nurse's station and meet us there if you like."

"Okay I want to go by the gift shop on my way up and pick up some balloons for her," said Diane.

"No Problem, we will see you soon."

Diane stopped by the gift shop and filled Krisette's room with balloons. Just as Diane was putting the finishing touches on what would be their home for the next week, they wheeled Krisette into the room and through all the pain she smiled when she saw the balloons that read IT'S A GIRL!

"Hello sweetheart, how are you feeling?" Diane asked.

"I'm in a lot of pain, but it was worth it. I love the balloons," Krisette whispered.

"I thought you would." Diane smiled.

TWO FACE

Moments later a tall blonde with milky white skin and a smile that could light up the night entered the room.

"Hello Mrs. Michaels, My name is Kerry and I will be your daughter's nurse. Dr. Thompson personally asked me to take good care of you both, so if you need anything please use the call button. She is restricted to bed rest and I will be in to change the catheter and check the antibiotics and whenever you need something for the pain just push this button and you will instantly feel some relief. So you just lay back and get your beauty rest my dear," said Kerry.

Every time Krisette would get into a sound sleep the nurse would come in to check her medication and if it wasn't the nurse she would wake up to her mother hovering over her.

"I'm sorry I keep interrupting your sleep, but I want you to be as comfortable as you can be. How are you feeling?" Kerry asked.

"Very uncomfortable," Krisette responded.

"Is that normal?" Diane asked.

"Yes Mrs. Michaels it is. She has a catheter placed in the new urethra to drain urine from her bladder and she also has a rod-shaped prosthesis in her vagina to help the skin lining of the vagina properly attach itself to the vaginal wall. Both will be removed in about five days so Dr. Thompson can see how she is healing. I'm doing my best to keep her as comfortable as possible," replied Kerry.

"Thank you Kerry, I will be sure to tell Dr. Thompson what an excellent job you are doing taking care of my baby girl, "Diane said.

"I'm just doing my job Mrs. Michaels," Kerry said with a smile.

Krisette felt better with each passing day and was excited about the possibility of going home soon.

"Good morning, how are my two favorite girls doing?" Dr. Thompson asked as he winked at Diane.

"That all depends on how much longer I have to stay in the hospital. Doc, I wanna go home," Krisette whined.

"Let me remove your bandages and see how well you're healing," he replied.

Dr. Thompson removed the bandages, the catheter, and prosthesis so he could see how well she was healing. Krisette cringed with each touch.

"I know this is uncomfortable for you Krisette, but it has to be done."

"I know, it's just the first time I have been touched that way," Krisette replied.

"Well after the awesome job I did, it certainly won't be the last." He laughed.

"Does that mean I can go home soon?" Krisette asked with excitement.

"Is tomorrow too soon? Everything looks great and is healing properly so I will have Kerry teach you how to take care of your vagina and I will prescribe some more medications for you to take home with you. I want to see you in a week to remove the stitches and once a week after that," explained Dr. Thompson.

⚥

"Thanks doc," Krisette replied.

"Yes thank you for everything doctor," Diane said returning the wink.

He smiled and exited the room.

"What was that all about?" Krisette asked.

"Just a little harmless flirting," Diane replied.

"Hello ladies, Dr. Thompson just told me that you will be leaving us tomorrow, so Krisette I've come to show you how to care for your vagina. The most important thing you can do to ensure the success of your surgery is to dilate every day. If this is not done it can result in the shortening of depth and width of your vagina. It may be painful the first couple of weeks, but it is very important in developing maximum depth and ensuring post-operative functioning of the neovagina. Please pay attention because if this is not done properly it can result in serious injury. This is a set of dilators and as you can see they vary in size. You will begin with the smaller one several times a day and gradually work your way up to the larger widths. The goal is to get to the larger ones and then it can taper off gradually," Kerry explained.

Krisette hung on Kerry's every word to ensure she did everything exactly how she was told.

"After dilation the wound should be gently washed in the shower with Hiliscrub followed by douching while you are seated on the toilet. Mix 5-10 ml of Betadine solution with bottled water until container is full. You are going to insert douche to full depth, squeeze and hold the container tightly as you extract the douche. Keep the wound dry and apply Betadine solution with cotton balls and apply Kemicitine ointment with a cotton applicator. If you have any bleeding, apply pressure with a dry cotton ball to the site for fifteen minutes. During the first week wear sanitary napkins or tampons and change several times a day due to normal vaginal bleeding during your recovery."

"Wow that's a lot to take in, but I will make sure Krisette does everything you just explained to us," Diane responded.

⚥

"No worries mom, I took in every word Kerry said," Krisette replied.

"Don't worry Mrs. Michaels I will give you everything you need as well as the instructions. I just feel it's better understood when it's demonstrated as it's explained," Kerry reassured them.

"Thank you so much Kerry. You have been a Godsend," Diane said.

"You are welcome, but as I said before I'm just doing my job," Kerry replied.

∞∞∞∞∞

The next day Krisette was discharged from the hospital and went home to start her new life.

CHAPTER FOURTEEN

Krisette did everything she was told and made a full recovery from her surgery with no complications. She was growing into a beautiful, confident young lady. In fact, so confident she wanted to return to Severna Park High School for her twelfth grade year.

"Mom I want to go back to Severna Park for my senior year," Krisette stated.

"What about Lauren? Suppose she tells everyone what happened at the sleep over?"

"That was three years ago and besides things have changed," Krisette said as she twirled around and struck a pose for her mother.

"They certainly have," Diane agreed. After seeing the excitement and confidence in her daughter there was no way she could deny her the chance of going to the senior prom and walking across the stage with her peers. With the exception of the few months Krisette went to Severna Park, she had been home schooled since the age of five. Diane made sure she learned everything she would have learned in a regular school setting and more. Krisette was very bright and Diane knew she wouldn't have any problems keeping up with the other kids. Since the surgery Diane didn't worry as much about Krisette being teased and from the looks of her no one would ever believe she was once a little boy.

∞∞∞∞∞∞

It was like déjà vu as Krisette walked down the hall on her first day back to school. All eyes were on her and just like before she was stopped by a very handsome young man.

TWO FACE

"Hello, my name is Derek, Derek McQueen and you are?" the young man stated extending his hand to her.

"Hello, my name is Krisette Michaels," she responded with a smile. Krisette was immediately attracted to Derek and not just by his looks, but his mannerism as well. Derek stood five feet, eleven inches tall, with a dark chocolate complexion. He sported a very neat regular haircut and sharply trimmed mustache.

As they stood in the hall getting acquainted Lauren appeared, only this time she wasn't coming to Krisette's rescue.

"Well, well, well what do we have here?" Lauren asked loudly trying to draw the attention of everyone in the hall.

"Hello Lauren," Krisette responded confidently.

"Oh you just gonna stand there and pretend like nothing happened," Lauren stated.

⚥

"I have no idea what you are talking about Lauren." Krisette rolled her eyes and gave Derek her full attention.

"Derek don't waste your time with her, she has a dick just like you," Lauren shouted.

Krisette stood there without even a flinch and waited for a reaction from Derek. Derek backed up with a raised brow and looked at Krisette from head to toe.

"Lauren, are you still upset because I wouldn't make out with you at your sleep over all those years ago?"

Lauren's face turned beet red as Krisette turned the tables on her. Everyone in the hall watched intensely as if they were watching a movie.

"I can show you better than I can tell you," Lauren replied. She walked over to Krisette and grabbed her by the crotch. Everyone's jaw dropped at Lauren's unexpected attempt to humiliate Krisette. Lauren stood there in the middle of the hallway fondling Krisette's genital area in search of a penis that no longer existed.

"Lauren I told you I'm not interested in you," Krisette said as she pushed Lauren away and walked away with her head held high. Everyone burst into laughter and this time Lauren was the one who ran away in shame.

"Krisette," Derek called out as he ran down the hall after her. Krisette stopped and turned to face him.

"Why did walk away from me, I thought we were getting acquainted."

"I saw that look on your face when Lauren made that ridiculous comment," Krisette replied.

"I admit her comment caught me off guard, but I didn't believe a word of it. How the hell could someone as fine as you be a dude?"

If only you knew, Krisette thought to herself. Krisette smiled and looked up at him with her big brown eyes. There was an instant attraction between them and neither of them could deny it.

"I would love to get to know you better," Derek said as he handed her a small card with his name and number on it.

Krisette laughed, "What are you doing with a business card in the twelfth grade. You don't have a business."

"First of all, I will have my own business one day, second, my dad told me to always be professional and third, I'm going to make it my business to make you my girl," Derek said with confidence.

Krisette didn't have much experience with boys, if any, but there was something very intriguing about Derek McQueen.

Later that day when Krisette arrived home from school, Diane noticed a glow on her daughter's face that she had never seen before.

"From the look on your face I guess I don't have to ask you how your day was," said Diane smiling.

"He's tall, dark, and handsome and his name is Derek McQueen," Krisette replied with stars in her eyes.

Diane chuckled, "Is that right? He must be a very special young man to have you glowing on the first day of school, but what about Lauren, did she give you any problems?"

"Mom, it's not just his looks, it's....just something about him," Krisette replied and handed Diane his business card. "As for Lauren, let's just say paybacks a bitch."

Krisette could tell by the look on her mother's face that she was impressed as well.

"Very impressive," Diane admitted handing the card back to Krisette. "Just take things slow sweetie. I don't want you getting too serious with the first boy you meet."

☿

"Ok, but the day I become Mrs. Derek McQueen don't get mad when I say I told you so."

The look she saw in Krisette's eyes was all too familiar as she had that same look when she first met Kristopher so many years ago. She decided to just listen and enjoy her daughter's happiness and if things didn't work out she would be there for her like always.

∞∞∞∞∞∞

Krisette and Derek had been inseparable since the first day of school. After Diane met Derek she totally understood the gleam in her daughter's eyes and saw it in his as well.

"Krissy, if it's okay with you and your mom I would really like to come over after school and talk to the both of you about something," said Derek.

"I'm sure it will be fine, but I will call her at lunch time to make sure she will be home. Why do I have to wait, can't you tell me now?"

"No Krissy, I want you both to be there together," Derek replied with a kiss on her cheek.

"Ok, I will see you later," she pouted.

When they arrived at the house after school Diane was just as curious as Krisette was. She wondered what Derek wanted to talk to her about.

"Hi mom," said Krisette

"Hello Mrs. Michaels how are you today?" asked Derek.

"I'm fine. I admit you have me curious about what you want to talk to me about." Diane responded.

"Yeah me too," Krisette yelled in the background.

"Ok well I won't keep you in suspense any longer. Mrs. Michaels, I would like your permission to take Krisette to the senior prom, that is, if she'll agree to go with me."

☿

They both screamed with excitement. "Of course I will go with you," Krisette answered with a wide grin.

Diane stood there in silence as she watched the two of them together and at that moment she knew Krisette was right, this would be the man her daughter would marry.

"Mrs. Michaels, is everything alright? May I take your daughter to the senior prom?"

"I wouldn't have it any other way," Diane replied embracing the two of them.

CHAPTER FIFTEEN

With less than a month until the prom Diane and Krisette woke up bright and early Saturday morning to hit every mall and boutique in Maryland and would cross state lines if they had to. They were both excited as they began their search for the perfect prom dress.

After hours of looking in every mall in Baltimore, Diane remembered this little boutique in Frederick, Maryland that she and her sister Cheryl use to go to when they needed something for a special occasion.

When they pulled up in front of the boutique Krisette smiled as she was impressed by the beautiful gowns displayed in the window.

"Good afternoon and welcome to Degala's," the woman said as they entered the boutique.

"Good afternoon," they said in unison.

"My name is Zara and I will be assisting you today. Is there anything special that you're looking for?"

"Yes, I'm looking for a dress for senior prom," Krisette replied.

"We have some beautiful gowns in the back, if you ladies would just follow me."

As they walked in the back Krisette saw something that stopped her dead in her tracks.

"Mom look," Krisette said as she pointed to the beautiful gown displayed on the mannequin. It was an elegant floor length pink chiffon mermaid gown with a strapless sweetheart neckline and the entire bodice was embellished with beautiful beads.

"Oh my God, that is absolutely gorgeous," Diane replied.

"This just came in today and it is made to order. How soon do you need it?"

"My prom is in three weeks," Krisette said.

"Let's go in the back so I can get your measurements and then I will see if we have enough time to order it," stated Zara.

Krisette was nervous to get undressed in front of someone other than her mother, but then she realized she no longer had to worry about her secret being revealed. She was a beautiful young woman with an hour glass figure.

"Ok we are all set and they can have your dress ready in a week, but we will have to do a rush order which is an extra fifty dollars."

"That's no problem Zara," replied Diane.

"Thank you so much mom, I can't wait for Derek to see me in that dress," Krisette said as they exited the boutique.

After accomplishing the mission at hand, Diane and Krisette headed for home.

☿

"Isn't this ironic?" Krisette said as Diane put the finishing touches on her makeup.

"What's that sweetheart?" Diane asked curiously.

"You use to get upset when I wore your make up and now you're putting it on for me," Krisette mentioned as she looked up at Diane and smiled.

Diane giggled, "Yes, I guess it is." Diane took a step back to take a final look at her daughter. "Sweetheart you look absolutely beautiful. I am so proud of the young lady you have become."

"Thanks mom, but none of this would be possible without you. You have truly shown me what unconditional love is and I love you for that," Krisette said with tears in her eyes.

"Girl, don't you mess up that make up." They both laughed.

"I never dreamed I could ever be this happy, but there's still one thing missing."

"I can't imagine what that could be," Diane replied.

"I wish you had someone special in your life. You put everything on hold to take care of me and to see to it that I was happy, but you need someone other than me in your life. I will be going off to college soon and I don't want you here alone."

"Well," Diane paused.

"Mom have you been holding out on me?' asked Krisette.

"Sweetheart the truth is I have been dating Dr. Thompson since you had your surgery."

Krisette's jaw dropped, "No wonder he agreed to do my surgery," Krisette smiled.

Ding Dong Ding... "Oh my God, Derek's here," Krisette said excitedly.

"Ok, I'm going to let him in and you can make your grand entrance in about five minutes," stated Diane.

⚥

Diane opened the door and Derek stood there looking handsome as ever in his black tuxedo with the pink cummerbund and bow tie that matched Krisette's gown perfectly.

"Come on in handsome," said Diane.

"Hello Mrs. Michaels."

"You look very handsome Derek."

Right on queue Krisette made her grand entrance down the stairs. The pink chiffon mermaid gown fit her body like a glove and accentuated her curves. The gleam in Derek's eyes was a definite sign of approval.

"I will be the envy of the whole school when I arrive at the prom with one of God's most beautiful creations on my arm."

God can't take full credit for this one, Diane thought to herself.

"You look very handsome Derek and I am the luckiest girl in school."

"You make a beautiful couple. Now let me take a few pictures before you leave."

Like any proud parent Diane got a little carried away with the pictures.

"Okay mom that's enough, we don't want to be too late," stated Krisette.

"Ok but it's not every day my only daughter goes to her senior prom. You kids have fun and be safe," Diane replied.

"We will, thanks mom, I love you."

About twenty minutes later they arrived at Martin's West with all eyes on them as they entered the ballroom. Every guy in the room had their eyes on Krisette and every girls were on Derek. They danced and mingled with friends, but Derek was ready to have Krisette all to himself.

"Baby, I have a surprise for you," said Derek.

"Really, what is it?" she asked.

"You will see in a minute," he replied as he took her by the hand and walked to the car.

"Where are we going?"

"Not far, but I need you to keep your eyes closed until I tell you to open them," he instructed.

Krisette did as she was told and kept her eyes closed. Suddenly she realized the car had stopped moving.

"Can I open my eyes now?" she asked.

"We are almost there," he replied as he led her by the hand. "Ok you can open your eyes."

When Krisette opened her eyes she was standing in a hotel room filled with candles and dozens of red roses. Derek took one long stem rose and handed it to her,

"Krisette, I want this to be our special night. I love you and tonight I want to make love to you."

Krisette stood there speechless. She loved Derek and wanted this as much as he did, but was afraid for obvious reasons.

"Derek, I love you too, but I've never been with anyone before and I'm scared."

"Neither have I but I want to share this experience with you. I feel in my heart that you will be my wife Krisette. Please share this with me," Derek said as he kissed her passionately and worked his way down to the nape of her neck as he unzipped her gown and peeled it from her body.

Krisette's senses awakened with each kiss as her body experienced pleasures unknown to her. She stepped out of her gown and exposed her hidden treasures.

"You are so beautiful," he said as he begins to undress. He then picked her up and gently laid her on the bed. He joined her and pressed his naked body against hers.

He laid there enjoying the sexy curve of her breast and firmness of her thighs. His fingers inched farther along the smoothness of her skin and stopped when it reached her clit. He kissed her long and hard while teasing her clit with gentle strokes of his index finger.

⚥

"Make love to me Derek," Krisette gasped with anticipation. He wrapped his fully erect member with a magnum and slowly entered her wetness.

"You feel so good," Derek whispered as their body became as one.

"Oh my God, I never dreamed of pleasure like this." Their feelings for each other emerged as they made love over and over again. This night was everything Krisette dreamed it would be and more.

Weeks later they both graduated at the top of their class from Severna Park High School class of two thousand and four.

They both attended University of Maryland Baltimore County (UMBC) later that fall with Krisette majoring in child psychology as she wanted to follow in the footsteps of the man she felt she owed her life to, Dr. Paul Stevenson. Derek majored in computer science with business as his minor.

CHAPTER SIXTEEN

Seemed like only yesterday Krisette was graduating from high school and now today she graduates magna cum laude from UMBC with a bachelor's degree in child psychology and a job waiting for her at The Center for Child and Family Therapy alongside her friend and mentor Dr. Stevenson. She wanted to help others as Dr. Stevenson had helped her, but no amount of education could compare to her life experience.

Derek also was graduating with a bachelor's degree in business and computer science with the dream of one day starting his own business. After being in a committed relationship since they met in high school, he was also ready to fulfill another dream he had which was to make Krisette his wife.

☿

After the graduation Derek and his family joined Krisette, Diane and Dr. Thompson for a celebration dinner at Ruth Chris Steak House.

"I would like to propose a toast to the graduates Krisette and Derek. I am so proud of the both of you. Krisette, you were truly blessed to find such a special young man at such an early age who loves you as much as Derek does. Derek, I just want to say thank you for loving my little girl," Diane said as a single tear ran down her face.

After Diane made her toast Derek stood up before Krisette and their families and made a toast of his own.

"Thank you Mrs. Michaels for your kind words and as far as thanking me for loving your daughter, I should be thanking you for giving birth to the woman I love with every beat of my heart."

Krisette sat there blushing and feeling somewhat embarrassed by Derek's words. After all these years she still couldn't believe how much he loved her, but often wondered would he still love her if he knew the truth.

"I love you too Derek," Krisette responded.

Derek got down on one knee and pulled a black velvet ring box from his right jacket pocket and said, "Then make me the happiest man alive and agree to be my wife."

Everyone stood in anticipation of Krisette's answer to Derek's proposal.

"Yes of course I will marry you." Derek put the three carat heart shaped diamond ring on Krisette's left ring finger. Everyone applauded and cheered for the happy couple as they shared a passionate kiss.

∞∞∞∞∞

Diane and Krisette wasted no time planning the most romantic wedding anyone had ever seen, but even with all the excitement Krisette seemed a little withdrawn.

"Krisette is something bothering you, you haven't been you self lately?" Diane asked with concern while making the final wedding arrangements.

"I've been thinking about something Dr. Stevenson said to me when I was in the hospital about the whole Lauren situation."

"What did he say honey?"

"He told me I should be honest with the people I love and if they love me it wouldn't matter that I'm transgender," Krisette stated.

"Sweetheart do you really want to risk losing a man like Derek?"

"No mom, but doesn't he have the right to decide for himself if he wants to marry someone like me," cried Krisette.

"What do you mean someone like you? Sweetheart you are a beautiful, intelligent, sexy young woman and unless you tell him he will never know the truth. Did he question your gender when you had sex with him after the senior prom?

"How did you know we had sex that night?" Krisette asked feeling embarrassed.

"Krisette I was a teenager once and that glow on your face the next day said it all," Diane replied. They both laughed.

"I guess you're right. I just pray I can live with this."

∞∞∞∞∞∞

Krisette and Derek decided to have a small intimate wedding with just family on a beautiful beach in Hawaii.

TRAE FERGUSON

You are cordially invited to the wedding of

Krisette Danielle Michaels

&

Derek Anthony McQueen

On

January 1.2009

At

Sunset

In

Pirate Cove of Oahu Hawaii

TWO FACE

Derek anxiously awaited his bride as the waves crashed dramatically into the large lava rocks in preparation for her entrance.

Krisette walked barefoot along the beautiful white sandy beach as the brilliant orange Hawaiian sun was going to sleep. She was as beautiful as the powdery blue sky above in a white sleeveless double faced satin gown with a draped cowl neckline and open back accented with a stunning crystal floral corsage and a sixty inch sweep train. The light breeze blew through her curly locks while a single pink orchid rested beautifully on the right side of her hair.

A single tear formed in Krisette's eye when she saw her handsome groom standing there in his white tuxedo and lei made of pink and white orchids around his neck. She joined him with their family surrounding them with love.

They looked into each other's eyes as they vowed before their family and God to love, honor and cherish 'til death do them part.

⚥

CHAPTER SEVENTEEN

Derek had everything he wanted, a beautiful wife, a beautiful home and a successful business, but there was still one thing missing in his life. Derek was ready to start a family. He was the only child and vowed never to subject his child to the loneliness he experienced as a child.

"Good morning sweetheart," Derek said waking Krisette with kisses.

Krisette turned and looked at the clock on the nightstand on her side of the bed. "I've got another hour left why are you waking me up so early?" Krisette whined.

TWO FACE

"I thought we could start working on Derek Jr. before you go to work today, "Derek stated while pulling her back in his arms.

"Honey I need to go to the bathroom," Krisette said running in the bathroom and locking the door behind her. "Oh my God, what I am going to do now," Krisette whispered. She decided to take a shower and hoped Derek would fall back to sleep.

When she got out the shower Derek was fast asleep. She quickly got dressed and went to see her mother before going into work.

"Good morning Sweetheart, what brings you by so early this morning?" asked Diane.

"Mom, I don't know what I'm going to do Derek is ready to start a family and I can't give him one," Krisette replied franticly.

"Why didn't you just tell him in the beginning that you couldn't have children Krisette? You didn't have to tell him the real reason why you can't, but that part is true."

☿

"I was afraid he wouldn't want to be with me because he wants a big family."

"Krisette you have to be honest about this because there's nothing you can do to change the fact that you are physically unable to have children."

"I know, but I'm so afraid he will leave me," Krisette cried in her mother's arms.

"Sweetheart, go home and talk to your husband and if he truly loves you he will understand. You can always adopt a child."

Afraid of the outcome Krisette decided not to follow her mother's advice and just enjoy the constant love making that went along with trying to make a baby that would never be conceived.

∞∞∞∞∞∞

"Krissy I noticed your late this month maybe you should take a home pregnancy test."

"Late, why do you think I'm late?" Krisette asked.

TWO FACE

"I haven't seen the wrappers from your maxi pads in the trash like I normally do this time every month so I was hoping that we were finally pregnant after all that good lovin' I've been giving you," Derek said as he grabbed her from behind and softly kissed her on the neck.

Krisette would buy Kotex and the same time every month Krisette would put the wrappers in trash to make Derek think she was having a period.

Shit, I completely forgot, Krisette thought to herself.

"I picked up a few tests from the drug store last week so here you go," Derek said while handing Krisette the home pregnancy test. He paced back and forth waiting for the results.

"I'm sorry Derek its negative," Krisette said with tears in her eyes.

"Baby maybe it's time we go to a fertility specialist,"

"Honey I'm sure it will happen when it's supposed to, but in the meantime we can have fun trying," she said trying to make light of the situation.

"I love you Mrs. McQueen."

"I love you too Mr. McQueen."

Months had passed and Derek was getting impatient and insisted that they make an appointment with their doctors to find out why they were having such a hard time getting pregnant. He made an appointment with Dr. Leonard Jackson at Chesapeake Urology and Krisette made an appointment with her gynecologist.

"Hello Derek, I'm Dr. Jackson," he said as he shook Derek's hand.

"Pleased to meet you Dr. Jackson," replied Derek.

"I've read your paperwork and I see that you're concerned about infertility."

"Yes, my wife and I have been trying to get pregnant for over six months now and I'm starting to get a little concerned."

"Has your wife been tested?"

"She is seeing her gynecologist as we speak."

"Ok good, first I want to go over your family and sexual history," stated Dr. Jackson.

"Both my parents are healthy and my wife is the only woman I've ever been with."

"We can do a sperm and semen analysis that will assess your sperm count, their shape, movement and variables. If the test comes back normal we will do it a second time for confirmation. Two normal tests are usually interpreted to mean that there are no significant infertility problems. We can set up an appointment for you to come back and do the semen analysis."

"Dr. Jackson I would like to get this done today if it's possible," Derek replied.

⚥

"I don't normally do the analysis the day of the consult, but if you can do your part its fine with me," Dr. Jackson said with a smile.

"Thank you doctor, it's important that my wife and I find out what the problem is."

"I understand Mr. McQueen, the nurse will assist you from here and as soon I get the results I will give you a call."

"Thanks again Dr. Jackson."

When Derek arrived home Krisette was in the kitchen cooking dinner. "Hello sweetheart, how did your appointment go?' asked Derek.

"It was fine; Dr. Manning gave me a complete physical examination and blood tests. I should have the results back in a few days," Krisette replied.

"I should have my results in a few days as well."

A week later Derek received his results from Dr. Jackson that his second semen analysis confirmed that there are no problems of infertility.

Ring. Ring. "Hello," Derek spoke into the phone.

"Hello Is Mrs. McQueen available?"

"No, she is in the shower. May I take a message, this is her husband,"

"Hello Mr. McQueen, this is Tina from Dr. Manning's office."

"Are you calling with her test results," Derek interrupted.

"What test results? She has missed both of her appointments," Tina replied.

"What do you mean she missed both appointments?" Derek asked angrily.

"Maybe I should wait and speak to your wife," Tina said and quickly disconnected the call.

Derek went upstairs to confront Krisette about the call he just received from Dr. Manning's office. Krisette was in the bedroom drying off when Derek entered the room.

⚥

"What's wrong honey?" she asked.

"Dr. Manning's office just called with some interesting news."

Krisette stood there like a deer caught in the headlights. "Honey I can explain."

"Yes, explain to me why you stood there and lied to my face about going to the doctor. You even went as far as saying you had a complete exam and blood work."

"Calm down Derek."

"Don't tell me to calm down. Tell me why you're lying to me Krisette I would have more respect for you if you would have just told me you didn't want to have my baby, but instead you let me go to the doctor's and have test while you did nothing, but lie to my face!"

"I would love to have your child, but I can't Derek," Krisette said as streams of tears ran down her face.

"Sweetheart if you go to the doctors they may be able to correct the problem."

"Just stop it Derek, they can't fix this!"

"Krissy I will take you to a specialist just tell me what the problem is," Derek said with tear-filled eyes.

"Derek I was born a male!" Krisette yelled out.

"What did you say?"

"I was born a male and two years before we met I had sex reassignment surgery,"

Derek fell to his knees in disbelief. His mind flashed back to the day they met and he remembered what Lauren said to him, "Derek don't waste your time with her she has a dick just like you do." Those words played over and over again. He became sick to his stomach as the thought of him being in love with a man crossed his mind. All the intimate moments that he once cherished were now making him physically ill.

⚥

"Why did you do this to me!" he yelled as he jumped up off the floor and wrapped his hands around Krisette's throat.

"Derek please, I can't breathe," Krisette whispered while clawing at his hands trying to free herself from his deadly grip as she slipped into darkness. Derek rocked her lifeless body in his arms as if he were rocking her to sleep. He tucked her in bed and gently kissed her on the lips. He then walked over to the closet, retrieved a metal box from the top shelf and removed his 9 mm glock. He loaded it as he walked back over to the bed and lay next to his wife. He gave her one last kiss and whispered in her ear, "I'm sorry my love I could no longer live with you and I can't live without you," he said as he put the gun in his mouth and pulled the trigger.

TWO FACE

Butterfly

My life has only just begun

I must face this cruel world

There is so much for me to learn

Every day I am changing a little

Experiencing new feelings as I grow

I am a butterfly

All wrapped in this cocoon

Two bodies trapped in one

What you see is not the true me

A reflection of He, but I am she

As each new piece of truth shows through

My father denies me

For the unconditional love I crave

I suppress the spirits force myself to behave

Inside my cocoon I cry

TRAE FERGUSON

This curse makes me long to die
I am a butterfly
Struggling to get out
I must shed the shell
For I am living in pure hell
I am a butterfly
Now free from my cocoon
Beautiful wings I spread
No longer must I hide
The beautiful girl inside
My evolution is complete
I can live a new life
No more pain, no more strife
I am a Butterfly

© *La Redeaux*

About The Author

Trae Ferguson is a native of Baltimore, Maryland who found her love for reading and writing at an early age. She started writing poems and short stories as a teen, but always dreamed of one day writing a novel. In 2011, Trae made her dream a reality with the release of her jaw dropping debut novel, Sweet 16. She took a softer, yet straight forward approach in 2012 with her book of short stories, which was written for teens, about teens titled Run, Tell That! She continues to address real issues in her latest novel, Two Face. Feeling the need to share the many true life stories only acceptable in the world of fiction, Trae is dedicated to being the voice of many.

☿

TRAE FERGUSON

www.ingramcontent.com/pod-product-compliance
Lightning Source LLC
Chambersburg PA
CBHW061945070426
42450CB00007BA/1059